# Meditations of a Healed Mind: Welcoming into God's Grace

## Prayers and Invitations

Wendel L. Miser with
James S. Miser, MD

For information about this title or to order other books
and/or electronic media, contact the publisher:

Two Sisters Writing & Publishing®
TwoSistersWriting.com
18530 Mack Avenue, Suite 166
Grosse Pointe Farms, MI 48236

ISBN:
978-1-956879-63-6 (Hardcover)
978-1-956879-64-3 (Paperback)
978-1-956879-65-0 (Ebook)

Printed in the United States of America

All the stories in this work are true.

Cover and Graphic Design: Van-garde Imagery, Inc.

Credit for author photos:  Mary E. Miser

# Dedication

I DEDICATE THIS BOOK to the many members, clergy, and support staff of the two churches my wife and I have attended in Northern Virginia for more than 34 years. The members of both Rock Spring Congregational, United Church of Christ of Arlington, Virginia, and First Christian Church of Falls Church, Christian Church Disciples of Christ, have helped lay the foundation for my Christian Faith, for my service to community, and for my meditations at the Table of the Lord.

In 1989, the Disciples and the United Church of Christ declared that "a relationship of full communion now exists between our two churches." The ecumenical partnership rests on five pillars of acceptance and cooperation: a common confession of Christ, mutual recognition of members, common celebration of the Lord's Supper/Holy Communion, mutual recognition and reconciliation of ordained ministries, and common commitment to mission.

I was a deacon at both churches for a number of years and became an elder at First Christian in 2014. At the Lord's Table, Jesus knits our forgiven hearts together in a new covenant with our Heavenly Father. We are held in Holy Communion with the whole of God's family.

My sincere wish for the members of both churches is this. Let our seeking rest on a foundation of prayerful surrender, our understanding rest on a foundation of knowledge, and our wisdom be provided by the Holy Spirit. Let our individuality rest on a foundation of assurance that we are created by our Heavenly Father, and our community rest on a foundation of gracious and honorable acceptance of our differences. Let our trust rest on the foundation of God's Holy Word and our assurance rest on the foundation of God's promises. Let our faith rest on the foundation of God's abiding covenant with us.

# Contents

# Foreword

MY RELATIONSHIP WITH WENDEL and Mary Miser began in 2001 when I became their interim pastor, and while Mary was suffering through a cancer diagnosis and treatment. Wendel, as Mary's caregiver, was loving, attentive, and fully committed to her healing and wholeness. My memory recalls a very tender and concerned husband who would do anything for his Mary, loving Mary as she needed and beyond. Our prayers were deep and full. I fell in love with both as I witnessed them navigate the frightening terrain of Mary's cancer.

Imagine my surprise when I was told of Wendel's earlier dark and agonizing journey with schizophrenia. His healing had been so complete; his engagement on a personal level so gracious and empathetic. I could notice none of the scars of mental illness he and Mary had lived with for so long. A complete healing and living testimony to the marriage of superb medical treatment, unconditional love, and perhaps most importantly, a faith that was far more certain and tested than my own! I marvel at the power of Wendel's faith and his witness to the miracles of the living Christ.

This third book of the healing journey of Wendel Miser completes a personal and theological confession of faith: a life fully transformed by a fully integrated faith and life. The following pages present the theological confession of Christian faith that saved his life. Each invitation and prayer is a step into one of the myriads of ways that Wendel found, and continues to find, a joy so amazing, so fulfilling, and so perfect that he cannot keep from singing.

The Table of the Lord is home to Wendel and where he has been able to give voice to his gratitude. Each time he "comes to the Table," he shares his liberating, healing truth. He invites us to step into the mystery and ritual where "the past is over and gone" and the present is overflowing with the New Creation we can all become. For Wendel, the reality that Jesus Christ, as God's beloved and chosen, sacrificed his life for you, me, and the world… well that is almost too good to be true. Except that it is!

As Wendel's pastor for thirteen years at First Christian Church of Falls Church (Disciples of Christ), Falls Church, Virginia, I was able to walk with him as his life deepened in Christ. He became an elder in the church because of such growing wisdom, and he was able to express himself most eloquently at the Table where Christ meets us in Truth and Spirit. Savor each word and thought that follows. Allow Wendel's sacred experience in for a taste, and I know you will find that you, too, can "taste and see that the Lord is good!"

At the root of it all, Wendel's journey into wholeness is a love story: God, Christ, humanity, and the angels that took him for a dance with the Light of God. And this book is a gift of his love and his light.

With gratitude and thanksgiving,
Reverend Kathleen Kline Moore
Former Senior Minister
First Christian Church of Falls
Church (Disciples of Christ)
Falls Church, Virginia

# Introduction

IN THE YEARS I have been a deacon and elder in the church, I have prepared many prayers that express my love for God and my awe of His glory. All have been prepared for the benefit of the body of Christ as I have contemplated the wonder of His greatness. Many of these invitations and prayers were presented at the Lord's Table during Sunday services at First Christian Church of Falls Church (Disciples of Christ), Falls Church, Virginia, from 2014 through 2023. At First Christian Church, communion is served every Sunday by intinction. All are welcome to come to the Lord's Table as we remember our Lord and His sacrifice on the cross.

First Christian Church of Falls Church is a member congregation of the Christian Church (Disciples of Christ) that worships and celebrates the Lord's Supper as a spiritual focus. The Church believes in celebrating diversity and in outreach beyond the congregation. First Christian Church of Falls Church began our ministry on December 7, 1952. Our mission is to be and to share the Good News of Jesus Christ, witnessing, loving, and serving from our doorsteps "to the ends of the earth" (Acts 1:8). The Christian Church (Disciples of Christ) is a movement for wholeness in a fragmented world. As part of the one Body of Christ, we welcome all to the Lord's Table as God has welcomed us. Disciples have long been striving in the pursuit of Christian unity.

At First Christian, we are on a journey of faith as we seek God's presence and guidance for our lives. We are a community of faithful seekers, bound together in the love and grace of the One who is our Creator, Sustainer, and Redeemer. As members of the Christian Church (Disciples of Christ), we confess that Jesus is the Christ, the Son of the living God, and proclaim him Lord and Savior of the world. One of our most vital ministries is "Safe Haven," a drop-in day shelter for the homeless. We are a congregation that is caring, supportive, and loving of all God's people. First Christian Church of Falls Church is an Open and Affirming Congregation. We embrace all people at any point in their faith journey and recognize each person's spiritual gifts.[1]

Such Christian themes as thanksgiving, remembrance, sacrifice, mystery, unity, presence, and justice are emphasized as Christ speaks of forgiveness and a new covenant of love, justice, and mercy with the living God in His words at the Table as bread is broken, and cup is poured out.

I am home at the Lord's Table. I realize that I have walked from wilderness to His Table and that Jesus has saved me from myself and my own ways by His cross. Then, in the wilderness of my life, the Table was farthest from my experience; now, at the Lord's Table, I am home, home in a place where my past no longer is of consequence. At His Table, I am a new creature, welcomed home by the One who has saved me. I am coming to Him in covenant with God for a new way of living.

Now, He sends me back out into the world, confident that with Him, I will make a difference. At the Table, there is a community of love and faith in the way, the truth, and the life of Jesus, the One who is present with me on my journey in the world now and always. The bread and cup are for eternal hope in Him, who leads me on my way. I navigate the world while separate from it. I am at home with Him always while in the world only for a time. I am sustained by the body and blood of Jesus as I walk with God. In this way, my life now has purpose and meaning, made possible by my discovery and acceptance of Jesus as Lord of my life.

— Wendel L. Miser

# Chapter 1

# Invitations to the
# Table of the Lord

IT IS AT THE Risen Christ's own invitation to each of us that we come to the Table of the Lord to remember Him in simple gifts of bread broken and cup poured out.

These are the words of institution:

> 26 And as they were eating, Jesus took bread, and blessed *it*, and brake *it*, and gave *it* to the disciples, and said, Take, eat; this is my body. 27 And he took the cup, and gave thanks, and gave *it* to them, saying, Drink ye all of it; 28 For this is my blood of the new testament, which is shed for many for the remission of sins.[2]

As part of the one Body of Christ, we welcome all at the Lord's Table as God has welcomed us.

# Reconciliation

It is through the death of Christ that we are reconciled to God. So it is through Christ that we have received our reconciliation, that we have obtained access into the state of grace, that we enjoy peace with God, and that we rejoice in God. Reconciliation, grace, peace, and joy are all blessings that become ours only through the sacrifice and mediation of Jesus Christ. No wonder our prayers are offered to God through Him (Jesus), for there is no other way to the Father except through His Son, our Lord and Savior, Jesus Christ.[3]

Oswald Chambers once said, "When we are rightly related to Jesus Christ, human love is transfigured because the last aching abyss of the heart is satisfied. When once the relationship with God is right, the satisfaction of human love is marvelous."[4]

This Table of the Lord is where the full measure of God's relationship with us is nurtured. The Risen Christ invites all to the Table to enter into a new covenant with God. It is His gift to us. Jesus gave His life obedient to God in order that this gift could be realized in the forgiven souls of mankind. Let us pray.

# We Realize We are Saved by Believing

Paraphrased from Oswald Chambers' writings: We are not saved by believing, we simply realize we are saved by believing. And it is not repentance that saves us, repentance is only a sign that we realize what God has done through Christ Jesus. The danger here is putting the emphasis on the effect, instead of on the cause. Is it our obedience, consecration, and dedication that makes us right with God? It is never that! We are made right with God because prior to all of that, Christ died.

When we turn to God and by belief accept what God reveals, the miraculous atonement by the Cross of Christ instantly places us into a right relationship with God. And as a result of the supernatural miracle of God's grace, we stand justified, not because we are sorry for our sin, or because we have repented, but because of what Jesus has done. The Spirit of God brings justification with a shattering, radiant light, and we know that we are saved, even though we don't know how it was accomplished. The salvation that comes from God is not based on human logic but on the sacrificial death of Jesus.[5]

By our trust in Jesus, we realize we have been saved by His mercy on the cross.

We realize we are new creatures by the gift displayed at His resurrection. God's light appears when we recognize Him. Our storms pass when we trust, finally trust, and God's unlimited grace appears in sweet surrender. His answer comes when we pray. His love stays with us, and our joy is made complete by our companionship with the Risen Christ.

Gathered with His disciples long ago, it was at this Table, in the upper room, that, in the fullness of time, Jesus bestowed upon His Disciples a gift of forgiveness and a covenant of grace. At this Table, the same gifts await us.

The Risen Christ invites all to the Lord's Table. Come to the Table with your joy in the Spirit of life and peace. As we remember Jesus, come forward in new freedom. Come forward birthed in new hope, for the love God gives freely is yours. Jesus died for you to claim God's loving hold on you. Come forward to these gifts and be thankful. Let us pray.

# Carpenters

Carpenters are generally good at building homes.

Jesus the Christ, the architect of this and the wider church, is good at that sort of thing too.

All kinds of people are His building blocks, and unconditional love is His mortar for this living home of praise to God, our Heavenly Father.

Relationships with Jesus, His Father, and each other give the home its structure, and blessing is the door through which we are invited.

Abiding grace is the living space blanketed in the light of the Holy Spirit, where peace and harmony reflect its atmosphere.

The floor is anchored to a firm foundation, and above it is a roof secured in Heaven.

The design accommodates all people, and its floor plan was predestined from the beginning.

God's word is living water for all, and "Eternal Hope" are the words on the shingle that hangs above the door. At its groundbreaking stood a cross of sacrifice that guarantees this living home is paid in full now and evermore.

Built with promise, love, and commitment, a spirit of warmth, gratitude, and surrender has pervaded its sanctuary since its ordained founding.

In its center, in the midst of a spirit of thanksgiving to God, this, the Lord's Table of covenant and grace has been prepared with holy hands, where this morning, we remember and celebrate the presence of Christ. Our common understanding rests on the threshold of His love and His sincere welcome to all.

Here, for us, God's blessing of acceptance, mercy, forgiveness, and hope are manifested in simple elements of bread broken and cup poured out.

Jesus invites you to come forward to share in this, His everlasting covenant. Let us pray.

# Being in the Body of Christ

As many of you know, I'm a twin. It has been very comforting to know that I am an individual first but not separate from my brother, Andrew. God made us all individuals. Each of us is uniquely recognized as a separate and very special person. We come to Christ as individuals but enter into the one Body of the living Christ.

Each of us has an individual relationship with God, and as we are woven together as the Body of Christ, we recognize the cross as central to our lives in faith.

This Table of the Lord holds a central place for us as well. We will come to it, in a moment, as a community in unity and in communion, yet we will come to it one at a time, as individuals.

It is at Christ's own invitation to each of us that we come to the Table to remember Him in these simple elements of bread broken and cup poured out. As we come, we remember that this meal is a meal where we remember Jesus for what He experienced on the Cross: dying for our sin and, by His act, bestowing complete forgiveness upon each of us.

Likewise, at this same meal, we also remember Him as He walked on the road to Emmaus, where He appeared to those after His Resurrection. We also remember him in undying hope for our new lives in Him.

We remember Jesus today with great hope and joy, born in His death and resurrection for us.

The cross and this Table of our Lord are symbols of God's great love for us as individuals and as the body of Christ. We know that it is at this very Table that we are strengthened to go out as ministers of the Body of Christ, offering new birth into a living hope to each individual, one at a time. Let us pray.

# His Gifts of Giving

On that hill at Calvary long ago, for Jesus, His gift of giving was in His Holy state of dying, a gift to us as He held for us our redemption and forgiveness. As evidenced by the empty tomb, His gift of giving was in His rising, a gift to us in the unfolding of Holy grace within which our new life blooms in Him. Our joyful praise to Him in amazed recognition of these gifts is all we can do as we stand in the marvelous light of His victory at the cross and tomb. God's love for us is manifested by His Son's gift to us for our victorious saving.

The hand of God has prepared these gifts upon this Table. At the Table today, and ever-present, is the light that shines bright through the Risen Son in simple elements of bread broken and cup poured out. It is at the invitation of Jesus we come, and as we do so, the light of the living God is confirmed upon us. It is the light of faith, the faith to trust, the faith to seek, the faith to believe, and the faith to serve our God.

Our faith rests on the grace of the finished cross and the assurance the Lord gave to us by His sacrifice there. As we are strengthened here, we can know that what continually proceeds from such grace is covenant, promise, foundation, and redemption for our lives as we face the unknown.

Because of this grace, we can rest in the freedom and the fullness of eternal life. We can rest being renewed ourselves in the love of Jesus. We can bring love to others through the Spirit and bring hope to the world through relationship with our God. Out of such love and relationship, come forward. Rest in the knowledge that:

Prayers are answered; grace is bestowed,
Hopes are sustained, pardon is given,
Hearts are held, freedom is granted,
The hungry are fed, the truth is told,
Faith is strengthened.

Let us pray.

# God is Forever with Us

Today, as we come to this, the Lord's table, we come with faith, the faith to seek, the faith to believe, and the faith to serve our God.

Our faith rests on what happened at the finished cross once for all. And now, our spirits can soar as on the wings of eagles, and we can rest in the freedom and the fullness of eternal life.

We are renewed by the Son to bring His love to others and hope to the world by our relationship with God, the Father.

This morning, as we partake of these gifts of bread and wine upon this table, let us remember His sacrifice and His resurrection.

A friend of mine once told me that home is not where you are, it is who you are with, and that rich is not how much you have, it is who you have beside you.

Most profoundly, both truths are evident here at the Table of the Lord.

He awaits us here with a richness of grace that invites us to come to this table and trust in Him.

Come to His Table and rest at home. Let us pray.

## Joy at the Table

Today, there is joy at this Table. Our Redeemer, the Risen Christ, has set the Table before us with holy gifts of grace.

As we come to the Lord's Table this morning, let us remember now and always that these freely given gifts of bread and cup are given by God's Son, who died for us all for our healing and renewal.

So profound is His truth that we cannot begin to comprehend or understand the full measure of His cross of forgiving love, redemption, and reconciliation for us.

Come seeking Him.

Come to the mystery of this Table.

Be expectant. Come empty. And find Him.

He will bestow the truth of spiritual blessing and the blessing of spiritual truth.

Let us pray.

# Thanksgiving Sunday: Living Manna

With deep thankfulness this day, let us gather about this Table.
The hand of God has prepared it, our brother Jesus invites us to it,
And the Holy Spirit is alive in and around us as we come.

We come with faith and full of joy.
The Risen Christ meets us here with gifts of
His cup of salvation and living manna from heaven.

As these gifts are offered to us,
We treasure the Lord's presence with us
In which the living Christ is made known to us.

In sharing these gifts in thankful remembrance,
We experience afresh the assurance of God's great love,
And the kindness of Christ Jesus.

Here we receive new life.
Here we receive the bread of new birth.
Here we are called to follow and serve Him.

Come to the Table of grace and find all the love
Of this One who speaks of covenant,
And the promise of forgiveness for you
In the splendor of resurrection.

Here at this Table:
Let our seeking rest on a foundation of prayerful surrender and
Our understanding rest on a foundation of knowledge and wisdom
provided by the Holy Spirit.

Let our individuality rest on a foundation of assurance that we are created by our Heavenly Father and
Our community rest on a foundation of gracious and honorable acceptance of our differences.

Let our trust rest on the foundation of God's Holy Word,
Our assurance rest on the foundation of God's promises, and
Our faith rest on the foundation of God's abiding covenant.
Come home. Rest. And be with God. Let us pray.

# God is Reaching for Us

Long before the birth of Jesus, the living God was reaching for His people through the voice of prophets and saints of old. And then through the heralding call of an angel in Nazareth at the dawn of redeeming grace.

From the time of Calvary, He has been reaching for us through the cross of His Son.

Today, God is reaching for us as we come bearing our gifts just as the wise men brought gifts by the light of the star in the East, finding the babe lying in the manger.

Today, God is reaching for us through the teachings of Jesus and his Holy Word. He is reaching for us at our baptism, through the Holy Spirit, and in Jesus' name every time we pray.

As disciples of Jesus, God reaches for us where two or three are gathered in His Son's Name.

And as Jesus invites us to this Table this morning, come: Our Heavenly Father is reaching for us, waiting to embrace us and welcome us home.

Come and share elements of bread broken and a cup that is poured out for many: gifts that speak to us of His Son's loving sacrifice and His enduring relationship with us, an everlasting covenant.

Our Heavenly Father is here reaching out for us. Come forward and take the hand that is offered. Let us pray.

# Resting in New Life

The prophets of old foretold the coming of the gift of a savior.

It took the compassion of our Heavenly Father
to bless us with His Son, Jesus.

It took a bright star in the East
to guide us to Him.

It took a lifetime for Jesus to teach us
to come to understand.

It took betrayal
and His cross of pain to create a new life for us.

It took a stone rolling away and a stranger on a road breaking of bread for us to recognize the fullness of that new life and of our need for Him.

Come to this Table of grace where Jesus has brought us home to our Father. Find all the love of this one who speaks of promise and forgiveness for you in the splendor of resurrection.

Here at this Table:
Come home. Rest. And be with God. Let us pray.

## Our True Place in the Heart of God

As we remember Jesus this morning, He is ever-present with us, present at His invitation for us to come to His Table of grace.

By Jesus' crucifixion, God's Love was made manifest to us all by the complete forgiveness of our sins. We are forgiven. By incomprehensible grace, we have been returned to the living God in a relationship marked by a new covenant with His people. By Jesus' act, we can be at this Table in the right relationship with our God.

God's light does shine here, shining brighter than ever through the Son at this Table. Under such light, these elements of mercy give us a reality and a context of living in a new way:

> We are called to love God and neighbor,
> We are called to love our enemies, and
> We are called to truly forgive and to seek reconciliation in our lives.

With our spirits afresh, let us be as disciples on the road to the historic town of Emmaus, full of joy, for the Risen Son in our midst. The cross is now empty. Our Savior is not a stranger. He is alive and among us.

This morning, as if for the first time, we hear His words of institution from the gospel according to Matthew, and we are profoundly moved by the grace of body broken and cup poured out for our healing and new life in Him. The Risen Christ gives us our true place in the heart and hand of our heavenly Father, who ordained all of this for us.

Because we have been so profoundly forgiven, we can be a loving people, compassionate and ready for reconciliation with all.

Come to the Table living in Him. Let us pray.

# The King of Kings

The King of Kings, the Lord of Hosts, is hosting us to a banquet of grace and eternal life, where bread is offered for spiritual sustenance and cup is offered for a new covenant with Him.

From St. John 6:35:

"35 And Jesus said unto them, I am the bread of life: he that cometh to me shall never hunger; and he that believeth on me shall never thirst."[6]

Here at this Table, the living God is known in the breaking of the bread. As the cup is poured out and new covenant is bestowed upon us, His gift of eternal life is recognized once again.

Let us remember now and always that these freely given gifts were given by God's Son, who died for our healing and renewal.

So profound is God's truth that we cannot begin to fully comprehend the magnificence of His gifts of forgiving love, our redemption, and the ways reconciliation are open to us.

He blesses us here at this Table. Come with your understanding, seeking Him. Come to the mystery of this Table. Come empty and find. He will bestow the truth of spiritual blessing in everlasting ways. Let us pray.

# Victory Through Christ

What a blessing it is to be here at this Table this morning, where there is victory in the living God through Christ! The Risen Christ has set this Table before us with his gifts of grace. He invites us to it.

The invitation is for us to come home out of wilderness,
to leave burdens behind,
to discover second chances,
to find incredible new life,
and to experience true joy.

The invitation to a firm foundation in Christ
grounded in Him.

The invitation to a relationship with the one who
offers the promise of eternal life and a new covenant
with whom there is everlasting hope.

The invitation is lovingly offered for our healing.
Christ died for us on the Cross.
The risen Christ bestows forgiveness
on us for our sin, not His,
thereby purchasing our redemption
and our true freedom.

With this blessed assurance, let us pray.

# Easter Sunrise: Risen from the Tomb

As this morning's sunrise comes to Christians around the world, we see that the tomb is empty! Jesus Lives!

We have an awesome God! God knew that His Son, Jesus, was to confront the cross. In His sacrificial act for us, God promises the fullness of life to us.

Even Jesus promised His Disciples something beyond the cross at the Last Supper, an everlasting covenant within the Kingdom of God.

This morning, we see the first witness to these gifts. We enter the original biblical story in John's Gospel, where Mary Magdalene returns to the tomb after reporting the fact of the empty tomb to Peter and John. There, she stands weeping alone, and peering into the tomb, she discovers two angels in white, seated where Jesus' body had been, one at the head and the other at the foot.

As Mary turns away from the tomb, she sees a figure standing before her, but recognizing Him only as a gardener, she asks him where the body has been placed. In this moment, Jesus calls to her by name, and Mary responds, "Rabboni," which means "Teacher." Mary's devotion to Jesus expresses itself in an embrace. With a new joy, she goes to the Disciples and tells them that she has seen the Lord.

Jesus is resurrected, and the fullness of Life is here. In our response, let us trust Mary and her witness. God's love in all its fullness is here in resurrection splendor.

On another day, this Table might be at the foot of the cross; yet today, it is beside the tomb where the stone has rolled away.

Initially, emptiness would seem to be the point of the story. But it is not. Rather, this morning, the fullest expression of Life and Love everlasting is here for us at this Table.

The Table has been set, and the Resurrected Lord is inviting us to it. So, come. At this Table, the fullness of our joy has been made complete. Come and recognize the one who has risen from the tomb in the breaking of the bread. Let us pray.

# Easter Sunrise: There is No Loss in God

The tomb is empty! Christ is Risen!

We have an awesome God! God knew that Jesus was to be sacrificed on the cross. By the Glory of our Heavenly Father, Christ has been raised up from the dead.

And to our surprise, because of His Son's sacrificial act for us, the fullness of everlasting life begins here. We can now walk in "the newness of life."

It is what Jesus, himself, promised His Disciples at the Last Supper, an everlasting covenant.

This morning, we have our witness to these gifts.

As we have just heard from the biblical story in John's Gospel, Mary Magdalene, with new joy, goes to the Disciples and tells them that she has seen the Lord at the tomb.

This morning, God's love in its fullness is here at the Table in resurrection splendor. And the Risen Lord is inviting you to it.

These offerings of Bread and Cup upon this Table declare that where there is emptiness within the human condition, God's love will fill it.

Where there is sadness, God's love will make our joy complete.

Where there is loss, there is no loss in God.

And where there is loneliness, we can sup at this Table with friend and stranger alike to be as companions under the light of God.

At this Table, the fullness of our joy has been made complete. Come. Let us pray.

# Thanksgiving Sunday: The Language of Heaven

In recent days, many of us have prayed for the well-being of our nation, and we have remembered our blessings.

Let us pause for a moment and give thanks, the language of Heaven:

for small children at play in the rustle of fallen leaves,
for the beauty of momentary autumn sunsets,
for the cold crisp air we breathe, and for the sheer wideness of the wonderful sky as seen through branches of nearly barren trees,
for the approach of winter earth blanketed in crystals of white,
for the anticipation of a night star in the East coming to rest at God's command over Bethlehem,
and for the warmth of hearth and table
this Thanksgiving.

With gladness of heart, we take time to remember the boundless nature of God's love, the sanctity of human life, the gifts and sacrifices of our forebearers, and the bounty that flows from the blessings of our Heavenly Father.

During our rejoicing here, there stands this simple Table adorned with the gifts of Our Lord. The incomprehensible grace of God that He has bequeathed to us through our partaking of these elements remembers the events of Calvary.

Jesus invites you here. Come. As you come, rest in the full meaning of the cross of Christ. He laid His life down for us. In His great love for us, He died for our sin, redeemed us, reconciled us to God, and justified us.

On the firm foundation that Jesus has given to us, we can come to this Table as God's own beloved children. Expressed in these elements of bread broken and cup poured out, God's redeeming love is for you.

In remembrance of Jesus this day, we are in Holy communion with the whole of God's family.

Come, ye thankful people, come. Let God's love and overwhelming grace enter in and bring you home. Let us pray.

# Live into the Expression of the Will of God

Jesus gave Himself on a cross for our sake and, when resurrected, gave us the Holy Spirit through which we are able to experience the living God. The Trinity is the largest influence central to our lives. Our Heavenly Father's love awaits us here through the Lord's offering of these simple elements. This morning, as we have prayed the prayer Jesus taught us, we prayed for God's will to be done, not ours. As we come to the Table, let us live into the full expression of the will of God.

The Risen Christ invites everyone to the Lord's Table. The invitation of Jesus is an invitation to life in Him and through Him to a life with the living God.

From 1 Peter 5:10: God has called you to share in His Glory in Christ.

"But the God of all grace, who hath called us unto his eternal glory by Christ Jesus, after that ye have suffered a while, make you perfect, stablish, strengthen, settle *you*."[7]

The broken bread and the cup that is poured out provokes us to remember Jesus just as He instructed his Disciples to do so in the upper room.

Jesus compels us to believe and provokes us to love. In realizing true hope, we walk by faith beside him, who brings grace and peace to the world.

Our brokenness is healed by this Broken Healer; our weakness is brought to endurance by this one who endured the cross; and our despair and sadness are brought to profound joy in this resurrected One.

We remember Jesus as we break the bread
and share the cup, reflecting our life in God's abiding love.

Come to the Table and share God's love in peace and joy with your neighbor. Let us pray.

# The Hairs on Your Head

It is the Creator God who promises us:

"But even the very hairs of your head are all numbered. Fear not therefore: ye are of more value than many sparrows."[8]

"Thine eyes did see my substance, yet being imperfect; and in thy book all *my members* were written, which in continuance were fashioned, when *as yet there was* none of them."[9]

"Know ye that the Lord he is God: *it is* he *that* hath made us, and not we ourselves; we are his people, and the sheep of his pasture."[10]

"Behold, I have graven thee upon the palms of *my* hands; thy walls *are* continually before me."[11]

"Therefore, I say unto you, Take no thought for your life, what ye shall eat, or what ye shall drink; nor yet for your body, what ye shall put on. Is not the life more than meat, and the body than raiment?"[12]

"Fear thou not; for I *am* with thee: be not dismayed; for I *am* thy God: I will strengthen thee; yea, I will help thee; yea, I will uphold thee with the right hand of my righteousness."[13]

"But the God of all grace, who hath called us unto his eternal glory by Christ Jesus, after that ye have suffered a while, make *you* perfect, stablish, strengthen, settle *you*."[14]

"I have blotted out, as a thick cloud, thy transgressions, and, as a cloud, thy sins: return unto me; for I have redeemed thee."[15]

"A new heart also will I give you, and a new spirit will I put within you: and I will take away the stony heart out of your flesh, and I will give you a heart of flesh."[16]

Let us remember now and always that God's promises are secured and assured by God's Son, who died for our sins so that we might be forgiven, healed, and renewed. God has reconciled the world to himself in Christ, not counting our sins against us. God has called us to share in His Glory in Christ.

"10 The thief cometh not, but for to steal, and to kill, and to destroy: I am come that they might have life, and that they might have *it* more abundantly."[17]

"20 At that day ye shall know that I *am* in my Father, and ye in me, and I in you. 21 He that hath my commandments, and keepeth them, he it is that loveth me: and he that loveth me shall be loved of my Father, and I will love him, and will manifest myself to him. 22 Judas saith unto him, not Iscariot, Lord, how is it that thou wilt manifest thyself unto us, and not unto the world?  23 Jesus answered and said unto him, If a man love me, he will keep my words: and my Father will love him, and we will come unto him, and make our abode with him.  24 He that loveth me not keepeth not my sayings: and the word which ye hear is not mine, but the Father's which sent me."[18]

Jesus Christ invites all to the Lord's Table. We are held in the midst of blessing for what is given to us as we come. As we remember Jesus this day, come to where living Bread is broken. Come to where the sacred Cup of love is poured. Each one of us comes to the Lord's Table in relationship with God. As you come, listen for the voice of God's Spirit in your soul. Let us pray.

# Nails Did Not Hold Him

Long ago, at the heralding of a Holy One by Gabriel's cry, our Heavenly Father showered His great mercy and love upon the earth with the birth of His Son, a Savior whose birth signaled God's intention to release men from sin and despair to redemption and forgiveness.

We are now blessed with the limitless nature of that love and mercy shown to us by the cross Christ came to bear and with our Holy citizenship to gain a right relationship with our God to nurture and sustain.

The Roman authorities intended the cross and tomb to hold for their purposes, yet Christ came down from the cross and was not found in the tomb. Their original purpose had been thwarted in the face of God's Heavenly purpose, offering us redemption, forgiveness, and renewal for our lives. Jesus went to the cross, obeying His weeping Father and forgiving those who supplied the nails. God's love held him there.

At the Lord's Table, the body of Christ, represented by bread broken, offers us healing for our brokenness to our wholeness of being. And the blood of Christ, represented by the cup poured out, offers us covenant with Christ in a new way for us to be in Him dedicated to the service of mankind.

In concert with the eternal, our Lord's incomprehensible grace found here is real.

At the last supper, Jesus broke bread and lifted the cup with His disciples, instructing them to partake of the elements in remembrance of Him. Let us do the same. The joy found in following Him is what He wants for us. God's love is promised in the saving grace of our Lord Jesus Christ.

It is our realization of these Holy gifts that fills us with boundless joy, thankfulness, and prayer this day and forevermore. Let us pray.

# Our Lord Loves You and Me

As I stand here at the Table and survey these blessed elements, I am reminded with wonder and humility of the awesome majesty with which our Lord loves you and me in mercy and grace. Our Lord died once for all and is alive to us still:

> to reconcile us to God, that we might belong to him
> as His adopted,
> to bring us into relationship with God and teach us
> to love God with every fiber of our being and to love
> our neighbor as ourselves,
> to forgive us in full measure for our sin,
> to bring us to faith and keep us faithful,
> to give Eternal life to all those who trust in him,
> to free us from death as He dispels its shadow for-
> ever in eternal victory.

These, I know, are but a few of Jesus' many gifts that are embodied by this bread and cup for you and for me.

The living Christ invites you to the Table. At the Table, we are in intimate relationship with our triune God, a relationship for us to nurture and celebrate through the Son. We will show our love for God if we honor Jesus' teachings that have been set before us: love your God with all your heart, all your soul, and all your mind, and your neighbor as yourself.

Seek His Kingdom.

Keep His commandments.

Lean not on your own understanding.

Be not conformed to this world but be transformed by the renewing of your mind.

Be anxious for nothing.

Hope in the Lord.

Praise and serve Him.

Feed His people.

Hold onto what is good.

Do unto others as you would have them do unto you.

Show compassion and help the afflicted.

Forgive and be at peace with one another.

Share this bread.

Share this cup.

And remember our Lord this day.  Let us pray.

# The Root of Christian Love

Thomas Merton wrote: "The root of Christian love is not the will to love, but the faith that one is loved-the faith that one is loved by the Living God."[19]

From Mark,

"17 And he taught, saying unto them, Is it not written, My house shall be called of all nations the house of prayer? but ye have made it a den of thieves."[20]

And from Jeremiah is written of the Lord God:

"12 Then shall ye call upon me, and ye shall go and pray unto me, and I will hearken unto you."[21]

The Christian theologian, Oswald Chambers wrote: "By means of the cross, God undertakes to deal with our past. He does it in two ways: first, to forgive it, and then, he makes it a wonderful culture for our future."[22]

God does so because he first loved us. This is our God's promise to us. We can love God with our whole heart and our neighbor as ourselves because He first loved us.

The Holy Spirit is a seal of God's gifts in His kingdom through Christ Jesus. The apostle Paul grasped this image to describe the sealing of the Lord:

"13 In whom ye also *trusted*, after that ye heard the word of truth, the gospel of your salvation: in whom also, after that ye believed, ye were sealed with that Holy Spirit of promise, 14 Which is the earnest of our inheritance until the redemption of the purchased possession, unto the praise of his glory."[23]

The Risen Christ invites all to the Table. This invitation is given for our full participation in the mystery of God's love, a love from which we cannot be separated through Christ Jesus.

The elements here are for everlasting covenant with God and wholeness in our living in and through Christ.

At this Table, there is thankfulness for salvation, thankfulness for new life in resurrection, and thankfulness for wonder in our living.

As we remember Jesus, we honor the living God and cherish the love He offers each one of us.

As you come this morning, St. Francis of Assisi reminds us: "Hold nothing back of yourself so that …Jesus… who gives Himself completely for you may completely receive you."[24] Let us pray.

# The Tomb Has Been Discovered

The tomb has been discovered. The stone is rolled away. The linens inside are folded. We hear the tomb is empty, and we are gripped by surprise and fear. Empty! How could this be? We've all been there. Loss. The loss of a lover or a friend. A sudden death. A relationship in turmoil. We've all experienced it. Emptiness. The emptiness of feeling, the emptiness of promise, the emptiness of words. We hope for things to be different, for another chance at relationship, yet we do not recognize that stranger on the road we walk. Mary Magdalene was at the tomb, and she said she saw the Lord. We doubt. We walk for a while and return to the tomb. A Table stands not far from the tomb.

A Table like this one this morning. It has been set with bread and cup. We come from our homes and dwellings to be here this morning. But did we recognize the stranger we passed on the road? We know we should have taken time to notice or to ask about him because we know to entertain strangers for some hold angels unaware. Yet, it's the way we are feeling this morning: the tomb is still empty. We take notice of the Table that is before us, beautifully set.

We know now faith is necessary to believe the fullness of the Table in the light of the empty Tomb. The tomb's emptiness can be translated to our understanding if we dare to recognize the passerby. Only then does the Table have its fullest meaning. The one Mary saw is coming to this Table this morning to invite us to it. And if we dare to recognize Him, we will realize that we are with our Heavenly Father, and we will come to recognize the fullness of the Risen Christ.

Luke tells us that the Stranger is recognized when He "breaks the bread" on the road to Emmaus; the Stranger fills the emptiness with His presence, and Mary and Cleopas are at home with the Lord! They rush back to tell the others:

"And they said to one another, Did not our heart burn within us, while he talked with us by the way, and while he opened to us the Scriptures?"[25]

When Christ fills our emptiness, we are filled with his presence, indeed.

In profoundly recognizing the redeeming grace of our Lord Jesus Christ, our pain is recognized as necessary for our healing; our doubt is recognized as a need for faith; our lack is recognized as a need for our hope; our emptiness is recognized as a need for the fullness of life; and love is recognized for our saving. Come empty to the Table of the Lord and find the fullness of Life. The Risen Christ invites us here. Let us remember Him as we come forward. Let us pray.

# God is Smiling

God is smiling.
The heavens have opened.
And a star shines its light.
Gabriel rests.
Heaven's angels are singing.
The prophets have told of His coming.
God's Son has come.
Wise men are kneeling.
Their gifts are presented.
His Disciples waited upon his glory.
The watchmen keep vigil.
The world begins to know.
A shepherd brings a lamb.
The blessed shout for joy.
The meek come in trust.
The persecuted ask for protection.
The sinful, forgiveness.
The lonely, companionship.
The outcast, a home.
The lame, healing.
The children bring gifts of
Their laughter and play.
God is smiling,
His son has come.
And the world rejoices
While Mary holds the Son

Of God who has come to us
To save.

Our Risen Savior invites all to the Lord's Table. As we remember Jesus and His journey to the cross, let us gaze at this child of light whom our God sent for His purpose. Let us be as the three Kings and come bearing our gifts as songs of praise for this little one whose light is so bright, the glow of which will soften and warm the heart of the traveler who will search out the babe lying there. Manger light gives glow to hearts on the way to cross and tomb, resurrection light there to find. As you come to the Lord's Table, come also to Manger Light, where there is no shadow. See Him, who is the Light of the World, full of grace and truth. Let us pray.

# By the Time

Friends. By the time Jesus came to be with His disciples at the last supper, where He spoke of forgiveness and a new testament given through the elements, He had spoken God's Word to the world. He taught those who followed Him about the nature of God, and He told His Disciples that their faith made them well and they were justified by it. He told them that their joy would be profound, that they would be blessed as peacemakers, and that salvation would be theirs. This is true for us today.

As followers of Jesus, whether you feel like the woman at the well after meeting Jesus, or have witnessed the feeding of the multitudes, or have felt the Holy Spirit descending upon you, or feel that your sickness or deformity has been healed, you are being transformed by what you have experienced. Whether you have touched His garment, or have been as attentive to Him as Mary, or remain amazed to have seen Jesus at Emmaus, you are being transformed. Whether you are like new wineskins with new wine poured in, or reborn when you are old, or are becoming like Lazarus in spirit, or are like a caterpillar becoming a butterfly, you are being transformed into the image of Christ. In experiencing His awesome grace, love, and hope, you are becoming like Christ.

It may be that you are standing in His light for the first time. It may be that your eyes have been opened, and you are seeing things anew. It may be that your ears have been unstopped, and you are hearing His word afresh. Perhaps you're feeling the living hope of Jesus' forgiving act on the cross or eternal life in the resurrection of Jesus more profoundly. Whatever the case, you are being transformed into a new creature for His purposes through the imprint of God's living word. Follow Jesus, and you will become His very own at the delight of His Father.

The Risen Christ invites all to the Lord's Table. As we remember Jesus this morning, we are welcomed home by the One who has saved us. Come to the Lord's Table for forgiveness and for a new way of transformed living. Let us pray.

# The Stranger from Nazareth

It was on that first Good Friday that Jesus fulfilled God's plan, that God was to give His only begotten Son not to condemn the world but to save mankind. Easter is God's proclamation of this fact.

"3 Know ye not, that so many of us as were baptized into Jesus Christ were baptized into his death? 4 Therefore we are buried with him by baptism into death: that like as Christ was raised up from the dead by the glory of the Father, even so we also should walk in newness of life."[26]

By Christ's resurrection, we are held as new people with the realization of eternal life in Him, living for righteousness and being fruitful for God. God's love for us is steadfast and unconditional. This is the nature of God's gracious love. Our inheritance is imperishable, undefiled, and unfading. It is a divine gift, it is unchanging, and it is forever.

At God's welcome, the Risen Christ invites all to the Lord's Table. The bread and cup are symbols of God's love. They speak of Jesus' sacrifice and God's saving grace.

The bread and cup have been prepared with care. They are for you. As we remember Jesus, come forward "for a foretaste of things eternal."

Come, when you are fearful, to be made new in love.
Come, when you are doubtful, to be made strong in faith.
Come, when you are regretful, and be made whole.
Come, for there is room for all. All are welcome to the Lord's Table.

We are invited to come together around this Table as those who belong to the household of God through the Risen Christ. We are brothers and sisters who, in our baptized lives, live out the death and resurrection of Jesus.

Let us pray.

# It is Finished

In the many days of our Christian experience, our gratitude is a state of humble thankfulness. We are grateful for this Disciples of Christ Church and its relationship to the wider Christian church.

The gift that has been given is this:

Our new birth into the hope of the living Christ was promised to us when Jesus cried "it is finished" from the cross. It became eternal when Jesus was resurrected from the dead, and the face of the living God was made manifest: our relationship with God and our new life in Him given by the Holy Spirit.

This Jesus, who is the epicenter of grace, the cornerstone of peace, and the fountain of love, offers us an outstretched hand of hope for steadfast faith on our journey with the Heavenly Father, who is the only One who knows why we would tag along with His Son on this lovely ride.

The Risen Christ invites all to the Lord's Table. By His invitation, this morning, Jesus is letting us know that, by the Holy Spirit, the gifts of redemption, salvation, and eternal life are ours because we are His. Through His sacrifice, He has bequeathed to us:

A firm foundation upon which we can never be separated from the love of God, which is in Jesus Christ, our Lord;

A primary relationship with the loving God in which we have our being;

A relationship in which we are protected by God, and the world has no dominion over us;

And a relationship in which we can turn to God in prayer in the name of Jesus, and He will direct our way.

So come to the Lord's Table with hope. Come, find, and know that these gifts are yours. Let us pray.

# Look to Jesus Christ

In a past age, not far back from this present time, a cross and tomb did not hold the one who went there on our behalf. The Roman authorities intended the cross to hold Him. Yet Christ came down from the cross and was not found in the tomb. Their original purpose had been thwarted in the face of God's heavenly purpose, offering us forgiveness, healing, and renewal. The family of God has been reconciled to Him. In freedom and new life, we have been reconciled to the Father. It is because of God's loving sacrifice of His Son that God reclaimed His beloved family.

This Jesus, who holds the key to destiny's book, has kept it for you and me for our grace filled days from the beginning. He has done so for our growth to discipleship. He has done so for our learned response to His teaching and way. He cares too much for us to slip away down destiny's path without Him. What we have experienced in our lifetime, whether we know it or not, has been the will of God for us. We need but to recognize this fact and put our lives in His hand in such a way that ours will come to rest in His.

The Risen Christ invites all to the Lord's Holy Table. We come held by these Holy gifts, becoming new creatures in Christ's image for service to the world.

The bread that is broken for us offers us healing to our whole being.

The cup that is poured out for us offers us a new covenant with Christ in God. These elements are the marks of God's unconditional love.

In concert with God's eternal, our Lord's unlimited grace found here is real.

At the last supper, Jesus broke bread and lifted the cup with His Disciples, instructing them to partake of the elements in remembrance of Him. Let us do the same. Come forward in the true freedom that Christ offers. As we are amazed, let us be forever thankful for the gifts that have been given. Let us pray.

# Hope is the Best Thing

"Jesus came to earth a little child.
How can we comprehend the love
That such a mystery contains?
Poor and meek and undefiled.
Ah! Could we ever understand it?
A little child to save us all.
Yes, Lord of all, He reigneth on high.
The Son of God came down from Heaven
in order to forgive our sin.
With hosts of glorious angels standing by
The Savior of mankind was born a man."[27]

Divine hope for humankind appeared at the birth of Jesus, which ushered our realization of the love of God. "And the angel of the Lord said unto them, 'Fear not: for, behold, I bring you good tidings of great joy, which shall be to all the people.'"[28]

"11 For unto you is born this day in the city of David a Saviour, which is Christ the Lord. 12 And this *shall be* a sign unto you; Ye shall find the babe wrapped in swaddling clothes, lying in a manger. 13 And suddenly there was with the angel a multitude of the heavenly host praising God, and saying, 14 Glory to God in the highest, and on earth peace, good will toward men."[29]

Hope is here, and hope is maybe the best thing. From the manifestation of Jesus' resurrection, we see that Jesus is alive. He is in our bosom, He is alive forevermore, and we have hope in eternal life.

The resurrected Jesus invites all to the Lord's Table. In the Gospel, according to John, it is written:

"16 For God so loved the world, that he gave his only begotten Son, that whosoever believeth in him should not perish, but have everlasting life. 17 For God sent not his Son into the world to condemn the world; but that the world through him might be saved."[30]

At this Table, we remember Jesus. We remember His sacrifice that has given us the reality of redemption. We look to His resurrection, which gives us the hope of new life in and through Him in God's Kingdom here on earth. "14 Glory to God in the highest, and on earth peace, good will toward men."[31] In these troubling times, may it be so. Let us pray.

# To Know We Possess Eternal Life

The Spirit of the One who taught you to pray, "Our Father which art in heaven," is within you.[32] You are not alone. Embrace the companionship. Surrender to the love you find there. And the peace surpassing all understanding will be yours in which your faith will grow into grace-filled living, evidenced by the hope that is within you. Follow His Spirit, follow Him. He and His Father are one, and you are His adopted. His companionship will make your paths straight, will comfort you, and will bring you joy beyond imagining. The door to eternal life and your Heavenly Father is open.

The Risen Christ is calling us to the Lord's Table, where we are held within the love of God by the grace of our Lord, Jesus Christ, through the fellowship of the Holy Spirit.

The Lord's Table, this morning, as with the Last Supper when Jesus first shared the bread and cup with His Disciples, offers us the gifts of Eternal Life and Covenant with our Heavenly Father through Christ.

The Risen Christ invites all to the Lord's Table. By His invitation, He is letting us know that the gifts of Eternal Life and Salvation are gifts of God through a new covenant with Him. As we remember Jesus this day, come to the Lord's Table; come empty with hope. Come, find, and know that these gifts are yours. Let us pray.

## Standing in His Victory

Let us reflect on the Lord's victory on the cross at Calvary
when He cried, "It is finished."[33]
Let us reflect on the victory of the open tomb,
where there is no loss. No loss in God.

Let us stand now in His victory and feel His presence,
His assurance.

Stand resurrected, stand with the Holy Spirit.
Imagine His defeat of loneliness, fear, despair,
doubt, sin, anxiety, darkness, and death.

At this, the Lord's Table,
your loneliness will turn to your becoming
an heir to His Kingdom,
your fear will be defeated by His steadfast love,
your despair will turn to joy,
your doubt will turn to rock-solid faith, and
your sin is profoundly forgiven.
Your anxiety will turn to blessed assurance and
you will stand in His marvelous light on His
firm foundation of new life everlasting in Christ.

Imagine the impact of the Lord's victory on you.
Feel deeply the thrill of it.
Feel deeply the assurance He offers.

You will reflect His victory in your
companionship with others,

in your love, mercy, and forgiveness of others,
and in living His truth for all the world to see.

We now stand awake with Jesus upon our hearts,
With the wind at our back. We live in His presence,
Dancing with the Lord; anywhere is home with Jesus.
Leaning on His understanding, He is the lamp unto our feet,
And we rise in newness according to His Word.

Jesus' redeeming act happened once, for all people. All of us have been redeemed through His merciful sacrifice of body and blood. The Risen Christ invites all to the Lord's Table. As we come and remember Jesus this day, we have been made victorious by His sacrifice. We acknowledge and partake in broken bread and cup poured out as a remembrance of His gift to us. For this, we are truly thankful.

Imagine now, the thrill of your standing
in the victorious embrace of your Savior
as He promised so long ago.

Let us pray.

## When Jesus Wept

"When Jesus wept,
the falling tear in mercy flowed
beyond all bound;

When Jesus groaned,
a trembling fear seized
all the guilty world around;

Tears on that dark and doleful night
when powers of earth and hell arose
against the Son of God,
and friends betrayed Him to His foes.

When Jesus wept,
the falling tear in mercy flowed
beyond all bound;

When Jesus groaned,
a trembling fear seized
all the guilty world around."[34]

Jesus went to the cross willingly at the command of God, the Father. And God wept for us. With this merciful act, Jesus died, saving our lives eternally and giving us our relationship with the living God. And we know it is our God who allowed this to happen. He is at work in us today. Our God will teach us in the same hour what to say to each other, for our humanity is bound up with each other. He is asking us to be like Christ.

We also know that our God speaks to us in our souls. For this reason, it is important that we live from the deepest part of ourselves and trust the depth of God's presence there when we are with each other and helping those in need. As the Risen Christ invites all to the Lord's Table, the elements have been prepared with loving hands. As we remember Jesus this morning, come to the Table of the Lord with the love of God in your hearts and a smile for others on your face. Let us pray.

# The Guest of Our Soul

Hear these words from the gospel of John describing what occurred after the Resurrection:

"19 Then the same day at evening, being the first *day* of the week, when the doors were shut where the disciples were assembled for fear of the Jews, came Jesus and stood in the midst, and saith unto them, Peace *be* unto you. 20 And when he had so said, he showed unto them *his* hands and his side. Then were the disciples glad, when they saw the Lord. 21 Then said Jesus to them again, Peace *be* unto you: as *my* Father hath sent me, even so send I you. 22 And when he had said this, he breathed on *them*, and saith unto them, Receive ye the Holy Ghost."[35]

When they heard this word of truth, the gospel of their salvation, and believed in Him, they were marked with the seal of the promised Holy Spirit.

And this is true for us. Jesus sent us this Advocate, the Spirit of Truth, to be with us forever. The Advocate, the Holy Spirit, will teach us everything.[36]

From Romans:

"11 But if the Spirit of him that raised up Jesus from the dead dwell in you, he that raised up Christ from the dead shall also quicken your mortal bodies by his Spirit that dwelleth in you."[37]

The Risen Christ invites all to the Lord's Table. The elements have been lovingly prepared. Through the incredible gift of the Holy

Spirit, Jesus bestowed all the gifts that are evidenced by His life, death, and resurrection upon us. The Holy Spirit is a seal of these gifts of God's love and kingdom through Christ Jesus. Through the Holy Spirit, we experience in ourselves, and in connection with others of this faith, the very presence and person of Jesus Christ. As we remember Jesus this day and are guided by the Spirit, come and partake. Let us pray.

# Taking Your Place

By God's Son Jesus taking your place on the cross, something new happens to you. Jesus' intention is to let you find God by His empty cross, save you, remake you, and give you to God as His adopted. Jesus wants to give you the life He has always wanted for you in a way that you will realize your place in His Father's plan, in His Father's Kingdom, and in His Father's eternal safety.

God will protect you from harm and love you ceaselessly. You will begin anew with the Holy Spirit as your guide. Prayer changes things for you as you ask in Jesus' name. Faith, hope, and love will be precious gifts you will come to know, with God's love being the greatest of them. You will stand in God's grace as you discover ways to engage with others in loving ways.

You will come to know the whole redemptive Life of God as you love Him with all your heart and others as yourself. Your past will be left to God's mercy, and you will walk into a future protected by God's providence as God holds your present moments in the palm of His hand. Jesus went to the cross to give you a loving relationship with your Heavenly Father.

As the Risen Christ invites all to the Lord's Table this morning, come take your place. The elements have been lovingly prepared. We are home at the Lord's Table. At the Table, we are new creatures. At the Table, we are welcomed home by the One who has saved us.

As we remember Jesus, come to Him for forgiveness. Jesus loves you. He always has and always will. We are now blessed with the limitless nature of the love and mercy shown to us by the cross Christ chose to bear: our Holy citizenship to gain a right relationship with our God to nurture and sustain. Let us pray.

# Everything Begins with God

In our reading from the beginning of the Gospel of John, we learn that:

"1 In the beginning was the Word, and the Word was with God, and the Word was God. 2 The same was in the beginning with God. 3 All things were made by him; and without him was not any thing made that was made. 4 In him was life; and the life was the light of men. 5 And the light shineth in darkness; and the darkness comprehended it not. 14 And the Word was made flesh, and dwelt among us, (and we beheld his glory, the glory as of the only begotten of the Father,) full of grace and truth."[38]

We also know that God's most gracious gift to us is revealed unto us through Jesus' act of sacrifice on the cross. God's forgiving love in all its fullness has come to us through His Son's sacrifice.

"3 Blessed *be* the God and Father of our Lord Jesus Christ, which according to his abundant mercy hath begotten us again unto a lively hope by the resurrection of Jesus Christ from the dead, 4 To an inheritance incorruptible, and undefiled, and that fadeth not away, reserved in heaven for you, 5 Who are kept by the power of God through faith unto salvation ready to be revealed in the last time."[39]

God's love for us is steadfast and unconditional.

The Risen Christ is calling us all to the Table this morning, where we are held within the love of God, by the grace of our Lord, Jesus Christ, through the fellowship of the Holy Spirit.

In Romans is the well-known statement by Paul:

"38 Nay, in all these things we are more than conquerors through Him that loved us. For I am persuaded, that neither death nor life, neither angels, nor principalities, nor powers, nor things present, nor things to come, 39 Nor height, nor depth, nor any other creature, shall be able to separate us from the love of God, which is in Christ Jesus our Lord."[40]

The bread and cup are symbols of God's love. They speak of Jesus' sacrifice and God's saving grace. As we come forward, let us remember our Lord. As we do so, let us remember the words of Paul:

"12:1 I BESEECH you therefore, brethren, by the mercies of God, that ye present your bodies a living sacrifice, holy, acceptable unto God, *which* is your reasonable service."[41]

That we might follow the will of God and love our neighbor as ourselves. Come to the Table as confident as Paul. God's love is here for us all. Let us pray.

# Welcoming Strangers

At the empty tomb, the resurrected Jesus is a stranger to Mary until she hears him speak her name, and she turns around and sees him standing there. Later, Jesus is also a stranger on the road to Emmaus. It is only after He breaks bread that He is recognized.

To all of us, the Apostle Paul's exhortation is this:

"19 Now therefore ye are no more strangers and foreigners, but fellow citizens with the saints, and of the household of God; 20 And are built upon the foundation of the apostles and prophets, Jesus Christ himself being the chief corner *stone*; 21 In whom all the building fitly framed together groweth unto a holy temple in the Lord: 22 In whom ye also are builded together for a habitation of God through the Spirit."[42]

The Bible teaches us:

"2 Be not forgetful to entertain strangers: for thereby some have entertained angels unawares."[43]

With hospitality, a relationship with a stranger can unfold within moments. This is what happened on the road to Emmaus.

Luke tells us that the stranger is recognized when He "breaks the bread" on the road to Emmaus. Mary and Cleopas are at home with the Lord!

"And they said to one another, Did not our heart burn within us as he talked with us by the way, and while he opened to us the scriptures?"[44]

In our recognition of the Risen Jesus in our midst, we are Resurrection people welcoming strangers and friends alike around the Lord's Table. The Risen Christ invites all to the Lord's Table.

At this Table, there is the breaking of the living bread of God for our healing and the pouring of the living cup for covenant in our remembrance of our Savior's sacrifice.

There is hospitality in grace, in the embrace of each other, the caring for the least among us, and our sharing in thanksgiving.

Come. Let us break bread together and share the sacred cup of love in fellowship.

As we come, let us remember Jesus "with wonder and thanksgiving for God's love that knows no end." Let us pray.

# The Fullness of God's Love

The Risen Christ invites you all here today. All that is here is given as gifts from God as an expression of His love for us. Let us remember now and always that these gifts were freely given by God's Son, who died for our forgiveness and renewal. So profound is God's love that we can only comprehend in living wonder the magnificence of His gifts of redemption and of reconciliation.

Here at the Lord's Table, the bread is broken for us and is given to us for our healing. The cup is poured out and given to us as a covenant with our God. By partaking of these elements, we recognize our continual birthing into the fullness of God's love that transforms us into newness of life.

Our emptiness is transformed by the breaking of the bread to life overflowing, our loneliness is transformed by the cup to divine companionship with our God, and our sadness is transformed into joy.

As we stay close to God, Jesus gives us a new commandment that we love one another as He has loved us:

"35 By this shall all *men* know that ye are my disciples, if ye have love one to another."[45]

As we accept what is offered here, our hearts rise to joy. These gifts give us new breath, new life, new hope, and new love. These Holy expressions of God's love are here for us.

As we come forward, let us remember our Lord. As we do so, let us remember the words of Paul:

"12 I BESEECH you therefore, brethren, by the mercies of God, that ye present your bodies a living sacrifice, holy, acceptable unto God, *which* is your reasonable service."[46]

Let us love our neighbor as ourselves. Let us pray.

# The Redemption of Us All

The Risen Christ invites all to the Lord's Table. This is what the Lord told Jacob recorded in the book of Isaiah:

"22 I have blotted out, as a thick cloud, thy transgressions, and, as a cloud, thy sins: return unto me; for I have redeemed thee."[47]

The Bible tells us that Jesus died on the cross as our substitute to redeem us once for all.

The Christian theologian, Oswald Chambers wrote: "The revelation of redemption means that Jesus Christ came here that by means of His death on the cross He might put the whole human race on a redemptive basis, so making it possible for everyone to get back into perfect communion with God. 'I have finished the work which you have given me to do.' What is finished? The redemption of the world. People are not going to be redeemed. They are redeemed. 'It is finished.'"[48]

On the hill at Calvary, the redemptive Hope of God for all mankind was shown to us sacrificially through the crucified Christ and then again on the road to Emmaus through surprised recognition of the Risen Christ in the breaking of Bread.

In the upper room, at the last supper, Jesus shared this meal with His disciples and spoke of the grace of forgiveness and everlasting covenant with God in simple elements of bread broken and cup poured out. In these merciful gifts, we can now live in the newness of life in God through the unlimited grace and peace of Christ Jesus.

Jesus is with us today to give us wonderfully new lives in relationship with the living God. As we recognize the source of the gift, the resurrected Jesus welcomes all to this Table to be in the presence of God.

So come and rest in the welcome of new life as we remember Jesus. Let us pray.

# At the Heralding of a Savior

Long ago, at the heralding of a Savior by Gabriel's cry, our Heavenly Father showered his great mercy and love upon the earth with the birth of His Son. A Son whose birth signaled God's plan to extract men away from sin and despair to redemption and forgiveness. We are now blessed with the limitless nature of that love and mercy shown to us by the cross Christ chose to bear, our Holy citizenship to gain with a right relationship with our God.

On that hill at Calvary long ago, for Jesus, His gift of giving was in His Holy state of dying, a gift to us for His holding our redemption, forgiveness, and grace. Evidenced by the empty tomb, His gift of giving was in His rising, a gift to us for the unfolding of Holy grace within which our new life blooms. Our joyful praise of Him in amazed recognition of these gifts is all we can do as we stand in the marvelous light of His victory at the cross and tomb. We now travel following the risen Lord with purpose, dignity, and excitement.

The Risen Christ invites all to the Lord's Table. The bread and cup at this Table provoke us to remember our companion in His time of the empty cross and the empty tomb whose walk on a long-ago road beside others surprised them to believe. Remembering our companion surprises us to believe and provokes us to love. In realizing true hope, we walk by faith beside him to bring grace and peace to the world.

Our brokenness is healed by this Broken Healer; our weakness is brought to endurance by this one who endured the cross; and our despair and sadness are brought to profound joy in this resurrected one.

Our redemption is by His act. Our new life is by His rising. We remember our companion as we break bread for truth and life, and as we walk with Him, we are surprised to believe in the way of our Savior's Abiding love.

It is our realization of these Holy gifts that fill us with boundless joy, thankfulness, and prayer this day.

As we come to the Lord's Table, let our belief in God be our belief in the God of our salvation. Let us pray.

# Once For All

This morning, the Risen Christ invites all to this Table. Bread and cup have been lovingly set. The Table of the Lord is open to all because of God's ordained purpose: On the cross, Jesus died once for all. Jesus did not make any distinctions or exceptions. He died for you, and He died for me. Despised and rejected among men at the time of crucifixion, Jesus did not forget us on His cross.

As we remember Jesus this morning, we can all come to the Table grateful for God's Son's path to our salvation. He obeyed His weeping Father.

By dying for us all, Jesus gave us redemption through His blood, the forgiveness of our sins.

By dying for us all, Jesus showed His love for us and canceled the legal demands of the law against us.

By dying for us all, Jesus showed the wealth of God's love and grace for us.

By His dying, we are justified, holy, blameless, and reconciled to God.

By Jesus' resurrection in everlasting hope, we have obtained eternal life.

And at the bestowing of the Holy Spirit, we can be witnesses to others concerning God's Kingdom.

For as Scripture tells us:

"16 For God so loved the world, that he gave his only begotten Son, that whosoever believeth in him should not perish, but have everlasting life. 17 For God sent not his Son into the world to condemn the world; but that the world through him might be saved."[49]

"3 Blessed *be* the God and Father of our Lord Jesus Christ, which according to his abundant mercy hath begotten us again unto a lively hope by the resurrection of Jesus Christ from the dead, 4 To an inheritance incorruptible, and undefiled, and that fadeth not away, reserved in heaven for you, 5 Who are kept by the power of God through faith unto salvation ready to be revealed in the last time."[50]

"10 But the God of all grace, who hath called us unto his eternal glory by Christ Jesus, after that ye have suffered a while, make you perfect, stablish, strengthen, settle *you*."[51]

So many gifts. So, come. At this Table, God's love for us is deeper than we can imagine; His embrace of us is firmer than we can imagine; and His Heaven is closer to us than we all can imagine because of the cross of His Son. God's unconditional love through His Son awaits us at this Table. Let us pray.

# A Life Led by the Power of God

We become separated in darkness. We search and catch a glimpse there to discover our profound need for the Lord. We then seek him in truth but find Him seeking us even as we seek Him. We then discover and experience that we are never to be separated from our Savior nor the depth of His light. His love and grace in Holy embrace are truly the miracle of this life.

We need never know the plague of our own heart and the terrible possibilities in human life if we hand ourselves over to Jesus Christ.[52]

"23 And the very God of peace sanctify you wholly; and I *pray God* your whole spirit and soul and body be preserved blameless unto the coming of our Lord Jesus Christ. 24 Faithful *is* he that calleth you, who also will do *it.*"[53]

Come to the Table of the Lord, remembering Jesus, our Savior. Hand yourself over to Jesus and trust the Living God. Resurrection faith by God's power will be yours. Let us pray.

# God's Love is Made Manifest

The Risen Christ invites everyone to the Lord's Table. Let us come remembering our Lord Jesus.

On His cross at Calvary, Jesus mercifully made manifest the love of God for us all; a love from which we cannot be separated through Christ Jesus.

The apostle Paul, in 1 Corinthians, states:

"For ye are bought with a price: therefore glorify God in your body, and in your spirit, which are God's."[54]

In 1 Peter, we read just how high this price is for us:

"18 Forasmuch as ye know that ye were not redeemed with corruptible things, as silver and gold, from your vain conversation *received* by tradition from your fathers; 19 But with the precious blood of Christ, as of a lamb without blemish and without spot."[55]

These passages speak of our treasure in Heaven that, for us, is incorruptible.

We know this truth as we turn to Matthew's gospel, which teaches us the nature of what our relationship to God and our neighbor should be.

"37 Jesus said unto him, Thou shalt love the Lord thy God with all thy heart, and with all thy soul, and with all thy mind. 38 This is the first and great commandment. 39 And the second *is* like unto it, Thou shalt love thy neighbor as thyself. 40 On these two commandments hang all the law and the prophets."[56]

Your eternal treasure is here at the Lord's Table.

Jesus tells us:

"21 For where your treasure is, there will your heart be also."[57]

Come to where God's love is made manifest. At this Table, there is the breaking of the living bread of God and the pouring of the living cup, a covenant in remembrance of our Savior's sacrifice.

So come to the Table. Come to where your heart wants to be.

And bring your neighbor. Let us pray.

# Come, Ye Thankful People Come

Come, ye thankful people come. God's almighty blessings are all around us here.

Yes, His love is all around. And the Lord's Table has been set with care. Jesus invites you here.

Come as you are able. Rest in the full meaning of the cross of Christ and come to the fullness of His Table.

God's redeeming love expressed in these elements of bread broken and cup poured out is for you. Come, open to the mystery of it.

Our Brokenness is healed here. Our hope that is before us in the true life that Jesus gives is born here.

In remembrance of Jesus this day, we are thankful.

For each of us, Jesus' sacrificial love given to us through the Holy Spirit holds us forever in God's care. It holds us in Holy communion with the whole of God's family.

From here, each one of us can go forth today in the freedom of God's love, loving Him with our whole heart and our neighbor as ourselves.

Come, ye thankful people, come. Let God's love, in overwhelming grace, enter in. Let us pray.

# The Crossroad of That Long-ago Time

The crossroad of that time long ago at Calvary marks the centrality of the event, the cross of Christ for the world to witness then and for Christians today to remember at the Table of the Lord.

Here, in the breaking of the bread and pouring the cup, is our remembrance of sacrifice given for all for the forgiveness of sin. By this act and through God's great mercy, we are given the Lord's grace, peace, and His love's blessed assurance for spirit-filled lives.

From Romans, Paul puts this way:

5 Therefore being justified by faith, we have peace with God through our Lord Jesus Christ: 2 By whom also we have access by faith into this grace wherein we stand, and rejoice in hope of the glory of God. 3 And not only so, but we glory in tribulations also, knowing that tribulation worketh patience; 4 And patience, experience; and experience, hope: 5 And hope maketh not ashamed; because the love of God is shed abroad in our hearts by the Holy Ghost which is given unto us."[58]

The Risen Christ invites all to the Table of the Lord. He invites all of us to God's inner court. The foundation of the Table of the Lord is firmly laid at the foot of the cross of Christ.

As the Living God promises, Salvation and Eternal Life shine through Him, who died once for all. Here, God blesses us with all spiritual blessings in heavenly places in Christ.

As we remember Jesus and partake of this Holy meal this morning, we are acutely aware that these gifts have come down through the history of the Christian faith to this Table of Mercy, this Table of Eternal Life, this Table of Redeeming Grace, this Table of Unconditional Love, this Table of Living Hope, this Table of Everlasting Peace, and this Table of Unimaginable Joy.

So, come. As we remember Jesus, our Savior, and we thank Him for these gifts, come. He gives us a new everlasting covenant with Him and relationship with our God full of mercy and compassion. We are truly blessed. Let us pray.

# A Holy Table is Before Us

Praise be to the God and Father of our Lord Jesus Christ, who has blessed us in the heavenly realms with every spiritual blessing in Christ. For he chose us in Him before the creation of the world to be holy and blameless in his sight. In love, he predestined us for adoption to sonship through Jesus Christ, in accordance with his pleasure and will to the praise of his glorious grace, which he has freely given us in the One he loves.

"In whom we have redemption through his blood, the forgiveness of sins, according to the riches of God's grace;"[59]

A Holy Table is before us. An empty wooden cross is hung over the baptistry behind this table. Both are here for us to remember our Savior's sacrifice and our God's love given to us in everlasting splendor. Bread and cup are set before us, bread for new birth of true life and cup for everlasting covenant with the living God.

This, the last supper as Jesus is together with his Disciples, is, by Jesus' own lips, a foretelling of things to come for all of mankind. Jesus is telling us that in this simple meal that He died once for all; that by it, God's love is recognized; that a new everlasting covenantal relationship with the living God is embraced; and through Jesus' own resurrection, new life can be experienced.

In this sanctuary, I think it is significant that the Table is set in front of and the cross is hung above the baptismal tank where baptism is celebrated by emersion. This pool is where a celebration of our own baptism into the death of Jesus is held for us to come into the fullness of God's love and Jesus' mark of resurrection.

What gifts God, in His infinite mercy, have been bestowed upon us! The gift of His love and the gift of new life. This sacred meal celebrates them both.

The Risen Christ is here, and He invites you to this Holy Table. Let us remember Jesus, the gift that was given for us long ago, to partake in these gifts today.

Let us pray.

# In the Midst of Blessing

The beauty of our Heavenly Father's plan for our lives has been given to us through His Son, His Son's example, and His Son's life by way of miracle, parable, prayer, and sacrifice. His Son has gifted us the Father by His cross. And the Resurrected Jesus has gifted us the Holy Spirit from Heaven. Our Heavenly Father's plan is for us to live in communion with all in Heaven and on earth in peace and grace all the days of our lives if we but follow Jesus.

Victory has come to us in the Living God through Christ. This promise has come to us from God's Heavenly realm by way of manger, fulfilled on the cross and by an empty tomb and bestowed upon us through His blessed Holy Spirit.

The world has no dominion over us as we
Live with Jesus and
Experience the gifts of the Holy Spirit.

The living God's overwhelming grace is before us
For the joy of the living of our days and
For a faith in a future held by our Heavenly Father.

And the peace of God, which surpasses all understanding,
guards our hearts and our minds in Christ Jesus.

Christ Jesus invites all to the Lord's Table.
We are held in the midst of blessing for what
Is given to us as we come.

Our Heavenly Father shed His mercy
upon us by sending His Son in our place for the wiping
away of our sin by the sinless one. Jesus was sinless, yet on
that cross of shame, He took on our sin and died.
We have been spared and forgiven! For this, we remember him.
Here at the Lord's Table, bread broken and the cup poured out are
precious gifts of God's Son, who died for our forgiveness, healing,
and renewal.

So profound is God's truth that we can only comprehend in living
wonder the magnificence of His gifts of redemption and of reconciliation. We praise God for them!

In remembrance of Jesus, this day, we are held in Holy communion
with the whole of God's family. Faith, Hope, Love, Grace, Peace,
and Joy are ours. Our Father wants it to be. Let us pray.

# On That Calvary Hill

What a blessing it is to be here at this Table this morning, where there is true life for us in the living God through Christ!

The Risen Christ invites all to the Lord's Table with His gifts of grace. Bread and cup have been prepared for us by loving hands.

Let us come remembering Jesus' sacrifice for us all upon the cross. As we do so, we also remember the fullness of His life, and we are filled with wonder at His resurrection.

We are indeed witnesses to newness of resurrection light. Profound joy is ours in remembrance of Him, who lifts us from our circumstances to new lives of gratitude.

A poem in remembrance and joy:

At the crossroad of our redeeming grace,
And the world's affair with man's disgrace,
On that Calvary hill, so foreboding and dark,
A jeering crowd laid down their mark.

The Crowd's anger, an albatross,
Fixed our Savior to that cross,
His life offered up with nothing to hide,
Between two criminals, He suffered and died.

Now, the gifts upon this Table for the life on that cross,
He gave to us; there is no loss.
For today, He is the gift we celebrate,
He is risen and has opened the gate.

These elements laid upon this Table,
Are set with much love and hands so able.
Our Risen Lord is with us to sup,
As with bread and outpoured cup,

To give us our true life, so worthy
As we remember Him by His mercy,
So loving and free,
As He rose in victory from that tree.

So as to make forever plain,
Our steadfast place and glorious gain,
In Him who conquered death with life,
Leaving us His Spirit, we, no longer in strife.

Let us pray.

## Carrying Your Cross

The following story was told to me by a friend who heard the story by word of mouth over fifty years ago. It is a very common way we have come to understand carrying our cross while following Jesus. There was a fellow who was carrying his cross. After carrying it for a long time, he grew tired and couldn't carry it, and he went to Jesus. He said to Jesus: "I've grown tired of carrying the cross you gave me and can't carry it any longer."

Jesus told him: "Take the cross to the barn, go in the barn, and put the cross down. See if there is something you would rather carry on my behalf." So, the man went to the barn and opened the door. He went in and put his cross down. All he saw in the barn were all-manner-of crosses. Some big, some small, some very big, and some very small. Some heavy and some light. There were some with large nails, some blood-stained. Some with snarled wood and some with thorns. He was perplexed and could not decide what to do. Then he saw a cross in the corner that he thought might be manageable. He picked it up, and it was comfortable to carry. So, he decided to take that one and go back to Jesus with the good news.

"Jesus," he said, "I found one that seems reasonable." Jesus took a look at the man with the newly-found cross and said to him: "That cross is the cross you came to me with before you went to the barn."

In considering the cross we bear, we often think that it has to do with problems we face or illnesses we endure. However, Jesus wants us to realize that carrying a cross means carrying that cross for Him.

Carrying a cross means for us to trust in God's ways and to trust Jesus always. He said:

"27 And whosoever doth not bear his cross, and come after me, cannot be my disciple."[60]

The Risen Christ invites all to the Lord's Table. The elements here, this morning, are Jesus' body and blood shed for us in the saving grace of forgiveness and a new covenant with the living God through Jesus for our lives. As we remember Jesus, let us carry the cross Jesus gives us for the hungry, the thirsty, the stranger, the naked, the sick, and the prisoner. In this way, we will truly carry the cross Jesus means for us to carry.

"And the King shall answer and say unto them, Verily I say unto you, Inasmuch as ye have done *it* unto one of the least of these my brethren, ye have done *it* unto me."[61]

Come forward for life in the spirit of service. Let us pray.

# How Lovely is Thy Dwelling Place

How lovely is Thy dwelling place, whether it be on a firm foundation underfoot or rising to a cloudless sunlit day.

How lovely is Thy dwelling place on earth pronounced good by the living God: His creation for us to take care of as we live with God's bounty upon it.

How lovely are the tenets of Jesus' teaching or the life story of Jesus culminating at the cross and tomb. By the cross, Jesus has forgiven us, and He has given us a new covenant with God through His grace. Jesus came to earth to show us that God's Kingdom is here, and the Living God is here on earth for all of us through Christ Jesus.

How lovely is Thy dwelling place? Just look at your cleansed heart and your citizenship in and your being an heir to God's Kingdom.
You are children of God as His adopted sons and daughters.
You are saved by God's grace and reconciled to Him.
Your salvation and eternal Life are here
within the days of your life because of Jesus Crucified.
You are a new creature, and your new life has arrived because of Jesus Resurrected.

How Lovely is Thy Dwelling place?
Just live, look, and see!

Christ Jesus invites all to the beauty of the Lord's Table, where all these gifts are expressed for us by broken bread and cup poured out. As we remember Jesus this day, we are blessed beyond measure by these gifts for our lives. In reverence, we are drawn to service as Jesus teaches us to help the poor, the needy, the disenfranchised, the hungry, and the homeless. As we pray for their safety, let us share what we have and bring them, too, to this Table to see the living God through Jesus, the Christ. Let us pray.

# Details of Ordinary Life

We can be truly thankful at this Table of the Lord. It was at this Table that Jesus prepared himself with His disciples for what was to come to pass. Because of it, Jesus brought us all home to the living God, where we are encompassed by His magnificent and wondrous love.

Jesus is with us in the details of our ordinary life and also in the broad strokes of the extraordinary in all its wonder. This causes us to thank God for His Son.

Who else, if we go to Him in prayer, can smooth out the wrinkles of life or cause us to be amazed by it?

We are truly blessed that Jesus is with us in a relationship full of grace, where the smallest details of the ordinary won't confound us, while the greatest expression of God's Miracle won't overwhelm us in the moments of our lives. Let us all shout for joy and come to this Table.

His love is all around and holds us. We are home. Our Heavenly Father is here. The Lord's Table has been set with care.

He laid His life down for us, and in His great love for us, He died for our sin, redeemed us, reconciled us to God, and justified us. God's redeeming love expressed in these elements of bread broken and cup poured out is for you. Come, open its mystery.

In remembrance of Jesus, this day, we are held in Holy communion with the whole of God's family.

Let God's love, in overwhelming grace, enter in and bring you home. Let us pray.

# Declaration of Foundation

As Christians give thanks for bounty and blessing for the gift and sacrifice of our forbearers, there stands at the center of our faith a simple Table, a cross, and a tomb.

As we enter the life of our Lord here this day, with deep thankfulness, let us pause to remember.

The cross now stands empty. Jesus has risen from the tomb. We can only imagine what happened there and imagine His love with us still.

Jesus, now at the right hand of the Father, has turned our gaze toward Heaven and to each other—witnesses to the newness of resurrection light. Transformation from cross to Table sustains God's light at its brightest.

This Table declares foundation, grace, and mercy for our grateful lives. As the bread of life and His cup of salvation are lifted from this Table, we remember Jesus as He was lifted from a cross for the offering of true life and blessing.

As we accept what is offered, our hearts rise to joy. Profound joy is ours in Jesus, who lifts us from our circumstance. We recognize what He has given us for our life long.

Come to the Table of our Lord. His love is all around and holds us. We are home. Our Heavenly Father is here. The Lord's Table has been set with care. God's redeeming love expressed in these elements of bread broken and cup poured out is for you. Come, open to its mystery. Come, thankful people, come. Let us pray.

# Everlasting Hope

Today, at this Table of the Lord, as it was a long time ago, there is given to us an everlasting hope.

Remembering the last supper on the night of betrayal or the gathering on the road to Emmaus, everlasting is our hope at this present-day Table.

Your remembrance may be of the time of the crucifixion, an act that signaled profound forgiveness for all of mankind. Or it may be as you choose to be a part of the gathering at Emmaus, where you are one of a small group of travelers that found this hope again as they recognized the Risen Christ after breaking bread with the ones on the road.

Whatever the case may be, this Table embodies hope everlasting, enduring across generations. Our justification is as the people of God in relationship with the Him, in relationship with the Risen Son as savior, and in relationship with friend and stranger alike as a loving neighbor.

With this bread, He has said that, we will not be hungry, and with this cup, we will look to the saving grace of a new covenant with our God of love and commitment.

Come empty and receive the gifts. Come as you are. And be full of hope. These are gifts Jesus gave by free sacrifice for us all. Eat and live, then go and tell. Let us pray.

# Turning to Jesus

As one who was once lost and without a thought of Jesus, I now realize that I have come from wilderness to following Jesus to His Table and that Jesus has saved me from myself and my own ways by His cross. The Good Shepherd gave his life for me. In the wilderness of my life, the Table was farthest from my experience. Now, at the Lord's Table, I am home, home in a place where my past is no longer of consequence. At this Table, I am a new creature, welcomed home by the One who has saved me. I come to Him in covenant with God for a new way of living.

I can remember many years ago, turning to Jesus. As my relationship with Him grew, in a moment of wide-eyed realization and true thankfulness, I knew that Jesus had brought me home to my Heavenly Father. I knew, then, that Jesus was my window through which I could experience the sheer love and magnificence of the living God.

Jesus' way heals me so that I hear Him say, "Arise, go your way: Your faith has made you well."[62] I have found a song in my heart that I sing in thankfulness to God.

Jesus knows my need for my Father's mercy. And, through Jesus, in true joy, I know I can always turn to my Father. I have found a song in my heart that I sing in thankfulness to God.

Now, I know you are like me. We are home. Our Heavenly Father is here. The Lord's Table has been set with care. Love is all around. Jesus knows our need for our Father's mercy. And, through Jesus, in true joy, we know we can always turn to the Father.

Jesus invites everyone to the Lord's Table. As you come, rest in the full meaning of the cross of Christ. He laid His life down for us, and in the greatest love for us, He died for our sin, redeemed us, reconciled us to God, and justified us.

On the firm foundation that Jesus has given to us, we can come to this Table as God's own adopted children. God's redeeming love expressed in these elements of bread broken and cup poured out is for you.

In remembrance of Jesus, this day, we are held in Holy communion with the whole of God's family.

Come. Let God's love, in overwhelming grace, enter in and bring you home. Let us pray.

# Larger Than All Outdoors

The God we serve is "greater than all outdoors!" Fulton Sheen has said, "Creation is the work of God. Creation belongs to God alone."[63]

Christ's body was sacrificed to deliver us from sin so that we can live for our God through Christ. At this Table, His body is celebrated by the broken bread as a mark of our deliverance. We are free people through Christ's death. Paul preached to the Galatians:

"20 I am crucified with Christ: nevertheless I live; yet not I, but Christ liveth in me: and the life which I now live in the flesh I live by the faith of the Son of God, who loved me, and gave himself for me."[64]

Paul is telling us that this is true for us, too.

"3 For I delivered unto you first of all that which I also received, how that Christ died for our sins according to the Scriptures; 4 And that he was buried, and that he rose again the third day according to the Scriptures: 20 But now is Christ risen from the dead, *and* become the first fruits of them that slept. 21 For since by man *came* death, by man *came* also the resurrection of the dead. 22 For as in Adam all die, even so in Christ shall all be made alive."[65]

The Risen Christ invites all to the Lord's Table. We come to the Table this morning knowing we have a relationship with this creating and loving God whose son, Jesus, is with us through the Spirit.

The elements have been prepared with care. They are for you.

As we remember Jesus, come forward for a foretaste of things eternal.

Come, there is room for all. Let us pray.

# Our Place in God's Story

Here at the Lord's Table, our place in God's story is much more important than our place in history. Here, God wants a controlling interest in our lives.

We may never be important relative to the ages of world history, but we are important to God in His story here and now.

From the time of Jesus' crucifixion and resurrection, this Table has come down through biblical history to offer us a way to become part of God's story and for God to become part of our story each day of our lives.

The celebration is here. At God's welcome, the Risen Christ invites all to the Lord's Table.

Bread broken and sacred cup poured out are symbols of God's promise of redemption and eternal life in the living of our lives in covenant with the Risen Christ. God's love is here.

Jesus wants to show us the miracle of God's intention to give us lives full of grace and peace as His adopted children. Free to follow the living Jesus, we are asked:

"He hath showed thee, O man, what *is* good; and what does the Lord require of thee, but to do justly, and to love mercy, and to walk humbly with thy God?"[66]

In prayer, Jesus instructs us to do God's will and by His example, to embrace the poor, hungry, homeless, and less fortunate in God's love.

As we remember Jesus this day, come, let God make you a part of His story. Let Him be a part of your story. Leave the world's history behind. Come forward folded in God's eternal love, a fellow citizen of His household. Let us pray.

# The Greatest Love Story Ever Told

It was not until 1990 that I ended up in a church home. I had been searching for one for some time prior to that. Up until then, I was outside a church environment, and what I had learned of Jesus was from bible study, friends, books, and television. When I came to church, my learning of Jesus and His love accelerated in the months that followed.

Jesus is speaking of God's unconditional love for us. A trinity of love is given to us by God through His Son:

8 THERE is therefore now no condemnation to them which are in Christ Jesus, who walk not after the flesh, but after the Spirit. 2 For the law of the Spirit of life in Christ Jesus hath made me free from the law of sin and death."[67]

Since coming to church now for more than thirty years, hearing all the stories and parables of Jesus, I have learned this: while the world stands as a long climb toward economies and financial systems that support the rich, the ark of the love of Jesus bends greatly toward the disadvantaged, poor, hungry, and homeless.

The truth of Jesus and the reality of God's love for humankind is the greatest love story ever told. It is so because it is a transformational love that is given to us.

Behold this man, this Jesus, for He is the Son of God, resurrected, resurrecting men to serve His Father and His loving way. The life of love is unconditional, redeeming mankind for His purposes; each life is found to newness, purpose, and faith.

Come to the Table of the Lord and be fashioned into the body of Christ. Let us pray.

# The Lord's Omniscience

It was Oswald Chambers who wrote: "To believe that the Lord omnipotent reigneth and redeemeth is the end of all possible panic: moral, intellectual or spiritual... For a man to believe in the redemption means that no crime nor terror nor anguish can discourage him no matter where he is placed. God is not saving the world. It is done. Our business is to get men and women to realize it and we cannot do it unless we realize it ourselves."[68]

Jesus loves you. He always has and always will. He went to the cross to show you the beauty of God's love. The Risen Christ wants to give you the life He has always wanted for you in the Father's plan. Jesus knew His time on the cross would be worth it. By his crucifixion and resurrection, you are forgiven and recreated. These are His gifts for you. Your life is under the light of God's eternal providence. So:

"28 And why take ye thought for raiment? Consider the lilies of the field, how they grow; they toil not, neither do they spin: 29 And yet I say unto you, That even Solomon in all his glory was not arrayed like one of these. 30 Wherefore, if God so clothe the grass of the field, which to-day is, and to-morrow is cast into the oven, *shall he* not much more *clothe* you, O ye of little faith? 31 Therefore take no thought, saying, What shall we eat? or, What shall we drink? or, Wherewithal shall we be clothed? 32 (For after all these things do the Gentiles seek:) for your heavenly Father knoweth that ye have need of all these things. 33 But seek ye first the kingdom of God, and his righteousness; and all these things shall be added unto you.

34 Take therefore no thought for the morrow: for the morrow shall take thought for the things of itself. Sufficient unto the day *is* the evil thereof."[69]

Live by God's grace. Greet each passing moment by the will of God. Come to the Lord's Table in this moment of your faith and open your arms to the life the Risen Christ wants you to have with your Heavenly Father. Let us pray.

# Will We Be Recognized?

What a blessing it is to be here at this Table this morning, where there is victory in the living God through Christ! The Risen Christ has set this Table before us with His gifts of grace. He invites everyone to the Lord's Table.

This invitation for us to come to the Table of life is:

> To live within the true love of God,
>
> To rise from brokenness,
>
> To rise in true freedom,
>
> To live in faith,
>
> To see an open future,
>
> To find incredible new life,
>
> And to experience true joy.

We come to the Lord's Table to embrace a firm foundation grounded in Christ's sacrifice and to experience a relationship with the living God who offers us unconditional love and a life of living hope.

This invitation is offered for our healing.
Sinless, Christ died for us on the cross, paying for us a debt he did not owe,
bestowing forgiveness on us for our sin, not His,
thereby purchasing our complete redemption before God.

We now stand erect with Jesus upon our hearts.
With the wind at our back, we live in His presence,
Dancing with the Lord. Anywhere is home with Jesus,
Leaning on His understanding. He is the lamp unto our feet,
Our rising in newness according to His word.

At Easter, some years ago, Rev. Kathleen Moore described Resurrection this way:

It's like a caterpillar that has endured a metamorphosis, changing from one form into another, dying as a grounded creature, and emerging with beautiful wings for flight. She described the chrysalis of a butterfly as a symbol of the tomb in reference to Jesus' resurrection. A beautiful butterfly appears from the chrysalis in a short time. It does so as if its previous grounded life now appears never to have existed. After Jesus rose from the tomb, he was not initially recognized; however, He was subsequently recognized by Mary Magdalene by the sound of His voice, by Thomas seeing and feeling His wounds in the upper room, and by His disciples on the road to Emmaus in the breaking of the bread. Nothing short of miraculous!

And what about us? By example, the resurrection of Jesus allows us to be transformed into newly created creatures in the living God. The resurrection of Jesus allows us to be hopefully expectant about our future. I am sure that we will become more than able because of Jesus, even to fly as on the wings of eagles. We will have our own metamorphosis in the hand of God. And will we be recognized? Come to the Lord's Table and see. Let us pray.

# When God Measures a Man

For much of my time while growing up in my parents' home, there was a note on my mother's bulletin board that read: When God measures a man, He puts a tape around his heart, not his head. "His grace whispers to the heart that God's invisible work is enough."[70]

"The entire virtue of what we call Holiness lies in the faithfulness to what God ordains"[71] And, "God's grace will carry us well beyond the merits of our own actions where we will finally accept the pre-eminence of Holy love over human reason."[72]

In the beginning of the Gospel of John, we learn:

"In the beginning was the Word, and the Word was with God, and the Word was God...And the Word was made flesh and dwelt among us,"[73]

We also know that God's most gracious gift to us is revealed through Jesus' act of sacrifice on the cross. God's forgiving love in all its fullness has come to us through His Son's sacrifice.

"3 Blessed *be* the God and Father of our Lord Jesus Christ, which according to his abundant mercy hath begotten us again unto a lively hope by the resurrection of Jesus Christ from the dead."[74]

God's love for us is steadfast and unconditional.

The Risen Christ is calling us to the Table this morning, where we are held within the love of God, by the grace of our Lord, Jesus Christ, and through the fellowship of the Holy Spirit.

"28 And we know that all things work together for good to them that love God, to them who are the called according to *his* purpose. 29 For whom he did foreknow, he also did predestinate *to be* conformed to the image of his Son, that he might be the firstborn among many brethren. 30 Moreover whom he did predestinate, them he also called: and whom he called, them he also justified: and whom he justified, them he also glorified. 31 What shall we then say to these things? If God *be* for us, who *can be* against us? 32 He that spared not his own Son, but delivered him up for us all, how shall he not with him also freely give us all things? 33 Who shall lay any thing to the charge of God's elect? *It is* God that justifieth."[75]

This is the nature of God's gracious love. God has ordained it. It is a divine gift, it is unchanging, it is undefiled, and it is forever.

The bread and cup are symbols of God's love. They speak of Jesus' sacrifice and God's saving grace. As we come forward, let us remember our Lord, let us be faithful to what God ordains. Let us remember the words of Paul that we might follow the will of God and love our neighbor as ourselves:

"1 I BESEECH you therefore, brethren, by the mercies of God, that ye present your bodies a living sacrifice, holy, acceptable unto God, *which* is your reasonable service. 2 And be not conformed to this world: but be ye transformed by the renewing of your mind, that ye may prove what *is* that good, and acceptable, and perfect, will of God."[76]

Come to the Table of Jesus Christ as confident as Paul. God's love, which is in our Lord Jesus Christ, is here for all of us. Let us pray.

## Manger Light

Come to the glow of Manger light.
Looking directly at the baby Jesus
will cause you to see.
Jesus is the light of the world.

Come to Manger light.
The glow of it
will soften and warm the heart of the one
who will search for his relationship to the babe
lying there. The assurance
is the gift given from what has
come to be.

Baby Jesus shines his pure and
Holy light in the soul
so as to cause you to see His Father,
His kingdom, and His love unconditional.

For us, looking back to this Heavenly
ordained birth gives promise
to the miracle of our own rebirth as
His holy presence returns us to holiness.

Bethlehem's star gave light
to the wise men on the way
to the manger.

Manager light gives a glow to hearts
on the way through cross and tomb,
Resurrection light to find.

Once found, perceptions change.
Manger light is as bright as Resurrection
light at the moment of our realizing.

Come to where there is no shadow.
Come to manger light!
Look to Him and see!
Live in His light
for He is the Light of lights.

Ponder this life that God has given to
us, won't you?
You may find that the light of your rebirth
is as bright as God intends
it to be.

The Risen Christ invites all to the Lord's Table. Let us always remember Jesus, the Lord of our lives, at His birth, around this Table, and in our hearts, for the glow of manger and resurrection light is here. Rejoice and be glad in it. May it be so! Let us pray.

# Personalizing Our Relationship to the Universe

Sometime during my early Christian experience, I realized that Jesus was my window to the Living God. Jesus teaches us that God created the heavens and the earth and pronounced them good.

Now, The Big Bang theory to begin the existence of the cosmos has always suggested chaos to me. Yet, it must not have been. To me, the resultant cosmos and universe and the earth's place in it exhibits too many magnificent ordering principles in mathematical perfection to have been created in chaos. It is God who commands the orbital movement of the planets across the universe in grace-filled balance. He commands the rise and fall of the Sun across the sky with dramatic changes of light at the horizon. He commands the slap of waves at the edge of continents in sliding step. In summer, rhythm and harmony are displayed in a waltz-like dance of light, cloud, and breeze by day and glide of moon by night. Storms in spring can present as soft rain showers, cleansing the earth with instrumental gentleness, or in winter, as a twisting fury of wind, ice, and snow that stops the music. Creatures, large and small, move about the earth with percussive precision according to adaptive and hereditary plan. To one's eyes, God's orchestral symphony of earthly activity appears as a balanced kaleidoscope of cosmic movement and living dance across any landscape.

If a wholly majestic God is, indeed, around us and above us and is here holding the planets in a balanced dance throughout the universe, He must also be here holding us firm and giving us a place to acknowledge His wondrous works in all that He holds dear in this world. We must remember that His grasp of us is by the cross of His Son by which we are able to live, move, and have our being in the Son He has given to us. If we let our Heavenly Father hold us by the grace of His Son's merciful sacrifice, we will more easily understand and accept His awesome presence in our lives and His strength in holding the planets in place overhead. Our days, then, are held embedded in God's grace. We should never live and act without the knowledge of that fact. For if we forget our place in relation to God's grace, we will find our lives to be woefully out of balance with the Heavenly Father's desire for our lives. Even in our teetering, our Heavenly Father will continue to hold us; however, we will find no peace in our effort to balance until we acknowledge the one who gives us the grace to do so. Life is not a balancing act. As with the planets, rather, it is a state of balance. God's grace will leave us balanced on a firm foundation in order that we may live wholesome and productive lives and act in concert with His purposes.

The Lord's Table is before us. Our Heavenly Father's desire for our lives has been given by the sacrifice of His Son on the cross and is waiting in mystery for us here. Come and let God's grace hold you tight. Stand erect on the firm foundation He has given you. As you come, embrace your neighbor and be thankful for the many ways God has personalized this universe and Himself for you through His Son. Let us pray.

# Beyond Comprehension

Jesus, who has loved us beyond measure from before the beginning of our lives, chose a sacrifice His Father ordained for Him. This ultimate expression of His love for us is beyond our comprehension, a love so unconditional as to leave us blessed, amazed, and truly thankful for His sacrifice.

Jesus has brought us into a relationship with the Father by His cross. As a result, we can experience the gifts of the Father through the Son. Our Heavenly Father's plan for our lives has been given to us through Jesus, His example, and His life by way of miracle, parable, prayer, and sacrifice. Also, the Resurrected Jesus has given us the Holy Spirit from Heaven to be with us. Our Heavenly Father's plan is for us to live in communion with all in Heaven and on earth in peace and grace all the days of our lives as we follow Jesus.

We are blessed by what has been given to us as we come to the Lord's Table. As we accept what is offered, our hearts rise to joy. Profound joy is ours in remembrance of Him, who lifts us from our circumstance to recognize what He has given us. His sustaining and redeeming love embraces us as His cross now stands empty, the fullness of His kingdom for us to ponder.

"In Christianity, we find faith in which God wants a relationship with us. Man creates religions; yet God wants relationships."[77] "We have been invited to God's inner court."[78]

"Remember Whose you are and Whom you serve. Provoke yourself by recollection, and your affection for God will increase tenfold;

your imagination will not be starved any longer, but will be quick and enthusiastic, and your hope will be inexpressibly bright."[79]

We come to the Lord's Table one at a time as we experience Jesus, a gift upon the cross and gifts upon the Lord's Table, causing us to rise in truth to life everlasting.

Broken bread and the cup poured out here are precious gifts of heavenly sacrifice for our lives. We come at Christ's invitation, praising God for them! Light, Life, Love, Hope, Grace, Faith, and Joy are ours as the Father wants it to be. Let us pray.

# Do Not Fear

There are a great many "do not be afraid" verses in the Old and New Testaments of the bible. The one most recognizable to us all is Gabriel's cry to Mary, telling her she will give birth to a son in Luke 2.

From today's scripture in Matthew:

"25 And in the fourth watch of the night Jesus went unto them, walking on the sea. 26 And when the disciples saw him walking on the sea, they were troubled, saying, It is a spirit; and they cried out for fear. 27 But straightway Jesus spake unto them, saying, Be of good cheer; it is I; be not afraid. 28 And Peter answered him and said, Lord, if it be thou, bid me come unto thee on the water. 29 And he said, Come. And when Peter was come down out of the ship, he walked on the water, to go to Jesus. 30 But when he saw the wind boisterous, he was afraid; and beginning to sink, he cried, saying, Lord, save me. 31 And immediately Jesus stretched forth *his* hand, and caught him, and said unto him, O thou of little faith, wherefore didst thou doubt?"[80]

And this one from Luke's gospel:

"32 Fear not, little flock; for it is your Father's good pleasure to give you the kingdom."[81]

And from Psalm 23:

"4 Yea, though I walk through the valley of the shadow of death, I will fear no evil: for Thou *art* with me; thy rod and thy staff they comfort me."[82]

From John 14:27:

"27 Peace I leave with you, my peace I give unto you: not as the world giveth, give I unto you. Let not your heart be troubled, neither let it be afraid."[83]

From 1 John 4:18:

"18 There is no fear in love; but perfect love casteth out fear: because fear hath torment. He that feareth is not made perfect in love."[84]

These very familiar biblical passages are telling us not to fear. So many more passages are telling us not to fear. Jesus is here and has our back. God has given us his kingdom. And our lives are in God's hand.

The broken bread of life, which is the gift of Jesus' body broken for us, and the cup, which is Jesus' gift of his blood poured out for us, are blessed elements of God's faithfulness to us.

The crucifixion through the resurrection has ushered in new life; it has ushered in a peace that surpasses all understanding and unconditional love; and, for us, it has ushered in a profound love for the living God and neighbor.

So, step out in faith from the boat. Do not be afraid. Jesus is here. His mercy will catch you, and God's love will hold you. Stand still and see the salvation of the Lord.[85] Follow and give your will to Him. He will hold your burdens as you carry your cross. Pray to

Him, and He will listen and guide you. Step out of the boat. Jesus is here. He is close, and He waits for you to trust Him.

Let us remember Jesus and come rejoicing in His Spirit and not be afraid. Come to the Table of life and be at peace. Let us pray.

# The House of the Lord

Living in the house built by the Lord.
A key to every door
and rooms with no walls.

Celestial ceilings
painted with the color of life
and patterns of peace brushed
with everlasting grace.

His Son, the master window
to the Father's master plan
for the house large enough for all
who will turn to Him and trust His ways.

God's love is the light expelling the dark
from every corner, illuminating a forgiving space
for the living of every wounded soul.

Wounded from years spent within
perceived walls of mind and body.

Love strong enough to free the eye and ear
to recognize the purpose of His shelter
for healing to wholeness.

Walking from room to room,
each with its prayerful sounds
of assurance and mercy.

A welcome sign of eternal hope stands
at the front door of this, God's everlasting home.

All are invited to enter by a savior who went to a cross
in its front yard to redeem all who enter.

His Father knew the price and method of payment.
He loved us for its building.
A holy book has directions to it free of charge.
It will tell you of the way, the truth, and the life
of the one who is with you in the house of your dreams.

Living in this house built by the Lord.
A key to every door.
A resting place for every heart needing mercy.

And here, in the midst of Spirit, this morning,
stands the Lord's Table.

This Table of covenant and grace has been prepared with Holy
hands where understanding rests on a threshold of love and welcome is extended to all.

Here, for us, God's light shines brightest in the blessing of
simple elements of bread broken and cup poured out.

As we remember Jesus, this morning, come. Come with a prayer
asking for forgiveness of sin. Come home. Jesus invites you to come
to this Table to be at home. Let us pray.

## Life is a Mystery to be Lived

When I was a boy, my father said to me, "Son, life is a mystery to be lived and not a problem to be solved." I thought it curious that he said that to me because, at the time, his science was operations research, a science rich in problem-solving with industrial and military applications. I did not give it much thought, yet as I got older, I began to question his statement to me. What was the nature of the mystery? And what was it that I was to experience?

After finding and embracing Jesus in my thirties, I found through Jesus that the mystery to which my father was referring was the realm of my Heavenly Father. Further, our new birth into the hope of the living Christ was promised to us when Jesus cried "it is finished" on the cross. It sprang eternal when Jesus was resurrected from the dead, and the face of the living God and our relationship with Him were given through the Holy Spirit.

As we are separated from the world, a relationship with the living God is a way for us to live in the world while we heed the Word of God. A relationship with the living God through Jesus is a way for us to be ready to help the many people as God asks us to. It is a way for us to act toward the people we serve and a way for us to love our neighbor, stranger, and friend. It is a way for us to face hardship, tribulation, and pain and a way for us to pray in the name of Jesus to a God who will answer. It is a way for us to enter into communion here at the Table of the Lord and a way for us to walk with Jesus down the road of life to find true joy and to praise God for all the gifts He gives for our life long. It is a way for us to live in the world, blessing others.

Come to the Table of the Lord. These elements have been prepared with loving hands. In remembering Jesus this day, on a firm foundation as strong as grace, let us stand embracing the courage to step forward within the mystery of the living God to offer the world love, hope, and faith. We are the Lord's instruments, and through us, God is reaching for His people and bringing them home to Himself, setting their hearts ablaze with His love that has no end. God loves them for their saving. God has already ordained the gift. Let us pray.

# God's Light is Affirmed

There is an exalted God, the Creator of all things, who reigns over Heaven and earth and guides human events to accomplish His divine and good purposes. He does not change. He remains our fixed point. He is the one to whom we may turn at all times and in all circumstances for comfort[86]. His grace is your guide, and His mercy has your back.[87]

If we are honest with ourselves, we will recognize the truth and beauty of the situation we are in. We know God loves us because He sent his Son to the cross for the forgiveness of our sin.

God's light is affirmed and shines brighter than ever through the Son here at this Table. Under his light, these elements give us a reality and a context of living in a new way, where:

> We are called to love God first and foremost.
> We are called to love our neighbors,
> We are called to love our enemies,
> And we are called to truly forgive and seek reconciliation in our lives.

As we do so, we are asked to remember what Jesus did for us on the cross.

Knowing our sin, He loved us with an unconditional love and died for us to truly forgive us and reconcile us to the Heavenly Father. Here at the Table, there is a relationship with God to find, to nurture, and to celebrate through the Son. With such a relationship and Jesus at our side, come.

Let us pray.

# Be True

After my mother died some years ago, I had the honor of being given her 1943 journal that she kept the year before she was to be married during the Second World War. It was a religious journal, yet it contained other entries as well. Two of the entries were fascinating:

"Be yourself but make yourself worth being, speak for yourself but make yourself worth speaking, see for yourself but learn the art of seeing; seek for yourself but master the science of seeking." [88]

"Be true. Thou must be true thyself if thou the truth wouldst teach.
Thy soul must overflow if thou another soul wouldst reach.
The overflow of heart is required to give the lips full speech.
Think truly, and thy thoughts shall the world's famine feed.
Speak truly, and each word of thine shall be a fruitful seed.
Live truly, and thy life shall be a great and noble creed." [89]

Over the years I have journaled, I have discovered that if I am searching for God, I am searching for truth, and if I am searching for truth, I am searching for God. I believe that being yourself, being true, and being true to yourself is all part of the effort.

The following verses from the New Testament point to being true to God.

From 2 Thessalonians:

"11 Wherefore also we pray always for you, that our God would count you worthy of *this* calling, and fulfil all the good pleasure of *his* goodness, and the work of faith with power: 12 That the name of our Lord Jesus Christ may be glorified in you, and ye in him, according to the grace of our God and the Lord Jesus Christ."[90]

And Apostle Paul in Galatians:

"20 I am crucified with Christ: nevertheless I live; yet not I, but Christ liveth in me: and the life which I now live in the flesh I live by the faith of the Son of God, who loved me, and gave himself for me."[91]

"Jesus had a striking capability for understanding other people and discovering something fine in every person. He was not impatient with the mothers who came with their children on a busy day. He recognized no situation in which forgiveness should not be shown. He left no place in a Christlike life for grudges. He taught love for God and love for one's fellow man. When His teachings are followed, joyful relationships are found everywhere."[92]

The elements have been prepared with loving hands this morning. Here at the Lord's Table, the Risen Christ understands you. He invites you here to partake of the elements. As we remember Jesus this day, let us be true, true to His will, and true to ourselves. Let us come as fruitful seed in our search for truth and be ever mindful of our role in reaching other souls with the truth of Jesus Christ. Let us pray.

# Grace Happens

I remember the day in July 1995 when Mary's mother died. I had traveled down the street on an errand. The car in front of me displayed on its bumper a sticker that read "Grace Happens." In an instant, upon seeing it, I was graced by the memory of her life. Mary's mother died peacefully that day after a long battle with Alzheimer's Disease. I thought of her belief in the Lord and His impact on her life. As He promised to her, I imagined the sting of her death had been taken away by the grace of God. Until that day, I had not seen that bumper sticker. It was years before I saw it again.

On the second occasion, my mother had died the night before in December 2007. I had gone on an errand, and there it was again: "Grace Happens." Seeing the bumper sticker under those circumstances for only the second time left me to think of God's grace in a profound way all day long. My mother had died peacefully. God's hold on her delivered her home by His grace.

I learned earlier in my life that our fear of death is not taken away by our courage to confront it but by the grace of God:

"4 But God, who is rich in mercy, for his great love wherewith he loved us, 5 Even when we were dead in sins, hath quickened us together with Christ, (by grace ye are saved;) 6 And hath raised us up together, and made *us* sit together in heavenly *places* in Christ Jesus."[93]

Incomprehensible grace happens because of the cross. It is ours in this life because of Jesus' merciful death there. Jesus is our substitute on the cross, dying for the forgiveness of our sin and the bestowing of a new covenant and eternal life on us now and always. Eternal life starts now, continues throughout our lives, and at the hour of our death, we are carried within the love of God's grace through to life eternal.

At the Table this morning, we ask for God's blessing on these elements of grace, the bread broken and the cup poured out. We receive these gifts in remembrance of Jesus and His cross upon which His love was bestowed on us. These simple elements connect and unite us with God's history and His Son's journey to the cross. We partake of these elements not as a privileged few but as a humble people united with the whole body of Christ, mindful of our collective need for the incomprehensible grace of our Lord. Come and let the grace of our Lord happen to you. Let us pray.

# God's Ways are Not Our Ways

The miracle of life and Jesus' truth are reflected in our faith in God. Faith in and from God nurtures our hope. Jesus came down from the cross to walk along a road to change unbelief to belief, to rise to the right hand of the Father, and to bestow the Holy Spirit on the life of believers. Through this incredible gift, Jesus bestowed all of the gifts that are evidenced by His life, death, and resurrection. The Holy Spirit brings God's gifts to us.

The apostle Paul grasped this image to describe the sealing of the Lord:

"13 In whom ye also *trusted*, after that ye heard the word of truth, the gospel of your salvation: in whom also, after that ye believed, ye were sealed with that Holy Spirit of promise, 14 Which is the earnest of our inheritance until the redemption of the purchased possession, unto the praise of his glory."[94]

Today, His bestowing of the Holy Spirit on believers comes as Jesus is resurrected in Heaven. God's Kingdom is not of this world!

We remember the Lord, our companion, as we break bread for truth and life. Remembering our companion compels us to seek and to believe, provokes us to love God and neighbor, and to realize true hope as we walk by faith beside Him to bring grace and peace to the world. Our wounds are healed by this Wounded Healer, our weaknesses are brought to endurance by this One who endured the cross, and our despair and sadness are brought to profound joy in this Resurrected One. Our redemption is by His act. Our new life is by His rising. We are set in the valley of love and delight where He has bestowed the Holy Spirit upon us, and eternal life is before us.

We are now blessed with the limitless nature of that love and mercy shown to us by the cross Christ chose to bear. This is our Holy citizenship to gain the right relationship with our God to nurture and sustain. We now travel following our Risen Lord with purpose, dignity, and excitement.

"20 For where two or three are gathered together in my name, there am I in the midst of them."[95]

The Risen Christ invites all to the Lord's Table. Come to the Table and live.

Let us pray.

# Epiphany

Today, our Heavenly Father is showing us His great mercy and love upon the earth. The birth of His Son, a Savior, signals God's intention to guide men away from sin and despair to redemption and forgiveness. It took a bright star in the East to guide us to Him.

Until that ancient time, when the star stopped over the Holy child, all that was in the bosom of man was a hope of life. Under that star, the babe in the manger ushered in a new birth into a living hope, a radical reversal of a hope of life to a life of living hope. The divine love of the living God is here for us today in this baby Jesus. And as Jesus begins His new life, so do we. The evidence of this new life runs through all the stories of the New Testament of the Bible. His blessed hope is gloriously displayed for us today at His birth, through His lifetime, in His teachings and promises, in His experiences of healing the troubled people of His time, and in His gift of sacrifice on a cross. If you are moved, it could be that you are being transformed by a new birth into a living hope.

Whatever the case, you are being transformed into a new creature for His purposes through the imprint of His living word. Follow Jesus, and you will become His very own at the delight of His Father. Maybe this is what is meant to be foretold to us by the transfiguration concerning our inheritance in Jesus at Easter. The transfiguration demonstrates the purity of Christ and is the prelude to and evidence of the purity we Christians can experience through the transformative power of Christ's resurrection for us at Easter.

Our hearts are transformed, so let us bring our gifts remembering Jesus at His birth this day. Yet let us also remember Him as the child in the Temple, the Lord teaching in parable and lesson. He is the crucified risen savior who is here with us at the Lord's Table this morning.

It is at His invitation that we will partake in these elements of communion. We will break bread in remembrance of his body broken for all upon a tree. Also, we will be offered the cup symbolizing His blood of the new covenant with the living God, which is poured out for the forgiveness of our sin. Whether you are seeking, beginning to feel Him in your mortal bodies, or have felt him for a long time, remember, the Heavenly Father is fashioning you to be very much like His beloved Son, an heir to His Kingdom. Let us pray.

# Emptiness

Have you ever felt empty as an earthen vessel
When faced with:
The emptiness of feeling,
The emptiness of promise,
The emptiness of words?
Consider the fullness of cross and the emptiness of tomb
In profoundly recognizing the redeeming grace
Of our Lord, Jesus Christ:
Where pain is recognized as necessary for healing,
Where doubt is recognized as a need for faith,
Where hope recognizes the promise,
Where emptiness is recognized as the fullness of life,
And where love is recognized for the first time for the saving.
Come empty to the Table of the Lord and find the fullness of Life.

Let us pray.

# Environment of Faith

Stones are for tablets of Truth and seas are for deliverance.
Bushes are for burning and rain is for awakenings.

Rocks are for new waters and rainbows are for promise.
Stars are for the guiding and grass is for earthly time.

Stable animals and sheep are for a new birth of living hope.
Straw is for miracles and rivers are for the beginning of new life.

Mountaintops are for blessed sermons and clouds are for transfigurations.
Fish are for the journey to follow, and birds are for faith.

Valleys are for coming to terms with shadows and
Deserts are for overcoming.

Gardens are for joy and sorrow and
Hills are for light and sacrifice.

Palms are for adoration and
Grains and fruit are for covenant.

Trees are for forgiveness and salvation.
Lilies are for grace.

Doves are for Spirit and wind is for divine presence.
Vine is for family and evergreens are for eternal life.

Stones rolled away are for resurrections and
Heaven is for home.

Jesus' hand is for the holding and
Our journey is with Him on this road of life.

As we travel with Him, let us come to the Lord's Table of redeeming grace, unconditional love, and living hope. This morning, the Risen Christ is inviting us to this Table. As we remember our Lord, let us receive what is offered for covenant and forgiveness. As we do so, let us hold tightly to his hand of love. Our faith and salvation are safely in His hands forever. Let us pray.

# The Believer

As we come to the Lord's Table of sacrifice and love, remembering our Lord, we come to this Table. We are saved by God's grace and born from above; we are forgiven and offered living water; we are new creatures in Christ, reconciled to God and heirs to his kingdom; we are resurrected and conformed to the image of his Son. And with the Holy Spirit, we live with undying hope and eternal life.

These are God's promises to us through His Son's sacrifice on the cross. It was St. Simeon who said: "Faith is attainment of the invisible treasure of the knowledge of Christ." [96]

A friend of mine, Thomas Small, taught me that "Faith is the vault. The grace of our Lord is the door, and the love of God is the treasure."[97]

The apostle Paul grasped a similar image to describe the sealing of the Lord:

"13 In whom ye also *trusted*, after that ye heard the word of truth, the gospel of your salvation: in whom also after that ye believed, ye were sealed with that Holy Spirit of promise, 14 Which is the earnest of our inheritance until the redemption of the purchased possession, unto the praise of his glory."[98]

These promises of God are given to us as gifts of God, in love born out on the cross of Christ.

At this Table, God's promises are here, and we are blessed beyond measure. Come forward and receive these gifts by the breaking of bread and cup poured out. God gives them to us for new covenant and relationship with Him, full of mercy and grace. Let us pray.

# The Light of the World

The light of the world has overcome darkness. A resurrected life has overcome death. Christ's unconditional love has overcome hate. His cross of undying hope has overcome despair. The world has no dominion over us as we live within the gift of the Holy Spirit and experience the gifts of the Father through the Son.

God's overwhelming grace is before us. In thankfulness, we come to the Lord's Table in the presence of God's wondrous love for us through His Son. We are in the midst of blessing for what is given to us as we come to the Table this morning. The Lord, Jesus, invites everyone here to partake of elements of bread and of cup to remember the merciful sacrifice of our Lord.

His enduring love is present for us here:
For light and service,
For covenant,
For forgiveness of sin,
For foundation,
For birth into a living hope,
For the newness of life,
For gifts of compassion,
For God's reconciliation,
For love of neighbor,
For the beauty of the earth,
In stillness at dawn,
In wonder of the vast universe,
In sanctity of the present moment,

In Holiness of the ordinary,
Jesus has brought us home around this Table.

God's love at this Table holds.
It holds us in thankfulness for all these gifts as
We remember the Lord forevermore.

Bread broken and the cup poured out
are precious gifts of a merciful sacrifice for our lives.
We come at Christ's invitation, praising God for them!

Today, we are held in Holy communion with the whole of God's family. Faith, Hope, Love, Grace, and Joy are ours as the Father wants it to be. Let us pray.

# God Knits Us Together

When I was a boy growing into my teens, I would watch my mother knit a sweater or a scarf or a small blanket, and it would fill me with calm, warmth, and love for my mother. Many years later, working in Washington, DC, I would ride the subway and watch an occasional rider knit something while on the train. Most times, riding the subway felt cold, impersonal, and rushed as I traveled to and from work and home. Reminding me of my mother, these riders who knit on the subway put me at great ease during my journey.

Remembering both experiences, I am reminded of a favorite scriptural verse: "It is he that hath made us, and not we ourselves."[99] I often think of the Living God's great handiwork of knitting each one of us in our mother's womb. And then of all the knitting our God and our Risen Lord have done throughout our lifetimes. As we pray, God, through the Holy Spirit, knits our petitions and hopes together as we seek guidance for our lives. God's Living Word has knit the beautiful stories of manger, parable, cross, tomb, and ascension for our teaching and contemplation. God knits marriages and families together by His love. Strangers are knit together as friends finding common interests. Friends are knit together in common bonds of experience, love, joy, and laughter. Many workers are knit together while they labor together in a common pursuit. As Christians, each one of us is knit together into the Body of Christ around worship, love, and service to mankind.

First Christian Church of Falls Church has been knit together for many years, and our mission is to share the Good News of Jesus Christ, witnessing, loving, and serving from our doorsteps "unto the uttermost part of the earth."[100] God, through the Holy Spirit, has knit us into a tapestry of love in service to the poor, needy, hungry, and homeless. The Lord's Living Word moves us to commitment, service, and action. Many of us have found that, in working together, we have made a real difference in the lives of the less fortunate.

As part of the one Body of Christ, we welcome all to the Lord's Table this morning as the Risen Lord welcomes us. As we come, He knits us together into His Holy family by simple elements of bread broken and cup poured out. At this Holy Table, He knits forgiven hearts together in a new covenant with our Heavenly Father. Come and be a part of the Living God's handiwork. Come, be part of the warmth. Come, let your hands do God's work, embrace your knitting needles, and be part of His fabric of love. Let us pray.

# Cross and Table

In 2010, I was at a very special church service at First Christian Church in Falls Church, Virginia, where a large wooden cross was transformed into a simple wooden communion table. The juxtaposition of cross and Table left me in awe of the relationship between the Last Supper and the crucifixion itself, where I felt so graced in taking communion that day. I will always remember that day. After Christmas that year, I wrote this remembrance of the meaning of that day:

As the cross stands empty, Jesus rises from the tomb. He lives!

We, the mourners, have seen what happened there and imagine love with us still. Jesus, now at the right hand of the Father, has turned our mournful gaze toward Heaven, witnesses to the newness of resurrection light. The transformation from cross to Table sustains the light at its brightest. The Table made from the same wood declares foundation, grace, and mercy for our grateful lives.

His bread of life and cup of salvation are lifted from the table as He is lifted from the cross for the offering of true life and blessing. As we accept what is offered, our hearts rise to joy. Profound joy is ours in remembrance of Him, who lifts us from our circumstance to recognize what He has given us for our life long. His sustaining and redeeming love embraces us as we remember His sacrifice upon the cross, now standing empty; the fullness of His life for us to ponder His presence at this Table. We come to Him one at a time as we experience Jesus, a gift upon the cross and gifts upon the Table, causing us to rise in truth to life everlasting. As we look to the cross, we see the wideness of God's mercy for us through His Son. As we remember the tomb, we experience the fullness of God's love in the newness of our lives. As we come to the Table, we are offered both for the living of our days. Let us pray.

# The Victory by Way of the Cross and Tomb

As we come to the Table this morning, we know this: God loves us absolutely and unconditionally. We are forgiven by what Jesus did on the Cross. By his death, Jesus brings us back into the right relationship with God. Death has been swallowed up, and eternal life for us is given to us by Jesus' resurrection. We have eternal life in the present moment, grace-filled, and we are led through death to Eternal life with God. Eternal life in the present moment becomes precious and is a gift to those who seek and believe, and eternal life can be discovered for everyone by accepting Jesus into their lives.

Our lives in the present have been won by Jesus' death on the cross. In the present, God is with us through his bestowed Holy Spirit. In the present, the Holy Spirit within us is a gift of God from God. We have new life in Christ. The promise of God to us and the gift and the promise of the presence of the Lord forever has been fulfilled by the cross. Jesus becomes our window to our Heavenly Father through his life, death, and resurrection. He said, "My Father and I are one."[101] At Calvary, the crossroads of history, His story becomes our saving grace.

Now, man stands before the empty cross. Before God, are His redeemed people. Our past is spared by God's mercy. Our present is overflowing with His grace, and our future is held by God's providence. We are saved because we cannot be separated from His love. We are God's adopted. God's eternal design is impressed on this present moment, attending all that is within Heaven and Earth. At His crucifixion, Jesus told us, "It is finished."[102] The battle for our redemption has been fought and won for all time and eternity by God's Son, who went to the cross at the ordaining of our Father. Let us pray.

# Where Our Treasure Is

Let us come to the Lord's Table,
remembering our Lord Jesus Christ.
On His cross at Calvary,
He mercifully made manifest
the love of God for all.
It is a love from which
we cannot be separated
through Jesus Christ.

It speaks to us of our treasure in
Heaven, that for us is incorruptible.
We are to let earthly treasures go.
We know this truth as we turn
To Matthew's gospel, which teaches
us the nature of our relationship
to God and our neighbor.
"Thou shalt love the Lord thy God with all
thy heart, and with all thy soul, and with all
thy mind…Thou shalt love thy neighbor
as thyself."[103]
The treasure is here.

Jesus tells us that where our treasure
is, our hearts will be also. So, come
to where God's love is made manifest.
Come to where your heart wants to be.
And bring your neighbor. Let us pray.

# Chapter 2

# Communion Prayers

## Gratitude

Loving God, with gratitude for the elements upon this Table, we dedicate our lips to be the hopeful voice of Christ to the despairing, our hands to reach out in Christ's name to heal the broken, our feet to walk with Christ to visit those who are sick or shut in, and our bodies to be Christ's living sacrifice to break the power of death. As we come to the Lord's Table, be known to us now as we ask your blessing on these elements, your life-giving saving grace. Take us. Empower us. Use us. We ask in Jesus' name. Amen.

## East and West

Eternal God, Creator of all people...
You call us from the East and West and North and South
To feast at the Table of Jesus Christ.

In need of your mercy, strength, and love,
We come with grateful hearts for the loving presence of Jesus Christ
here in these spiritual gifts of bread and cup.

We humbly ask your blessing upon your Son's Holy gifts.

In our wonder of such blessing,
We come seeking newness of relationship with you and our neighbor.

We come asking for renewal of mind, body, and spirit
And the healing of our world.

We come expectant for the joy we yearn for within your eternal realm
And with thankfulness for your Kingdom to which,
You have made us heirs through Christ.

Whether we are gathered or scattered,
May we be the servant church of the servant Christ,
In whose name we rejoice and pray. Amen.

# Elements of Grace

Heavenly Father,
O God, you have created us in your image
And in Holy Communion at Christ's Table, today
We remember your Son through whom you effected
Our salvation and our reconciliation with you.

As we come, be known to us now as
We ask your blessing on these, your
Life-giving elements of grace.

With grateful hearts, we ask your Spirit
To grow us ever more perfectly into
The likeness of our Savior and allow your will
To work in us.

We give thanks for this gathered family of faith,
For this home, which tends, nurtures, and sends
Us out from this place in peace
To do your will in the neighborhoods of the world
Bringing the people there closer to you.

We ask this in the name of your Son, Jesus. Amen.[104]

# Gaining True Freedom

Heavenly Father:

We humbly ask your blessing upon us
As we partake of your Son's gifts of bread and cup.

As we do so, we remember it was by your Son's
Gracious sacrifice and victorious resurrection
That we have gained true freedom

A salvation marked by a new relationship
With you through the Risen Christ,
Who bestows upon us,
A complete forgiveness
And Spirit of life and peace.

Gathered with his Disciples long ago,
It was at this Table, in the upper room, that,
He bestowed upon them these same gifts of covenant full of grace.

We come with thankfulness for your Kingdom to which,
You have made us heirs through Christ.

We praise you in the name of your Son, Jesus. Amen.

# Gifts of Renewal

Loving God:

Thank you for your Son, Jesus, who has set a Table before us with His gifts of renewal. We ask for your blessing upon this bread and this cup. Let us remember that by them, we are forgiven in a most profound and gracious way. We are called to be salt of the earth and as light to the world. Being so, we can return our love to you and neighbor, and we can be stretched to reach out to the less fortunate among us.

Let us share what we have with those who are hungry, cold, and alone. You have entrusted to us a sacred call to share the good news of your Kingdom with others. To this Table, we come asking for strength to do so. We ask this in the name of your Son, Jesus. Amen.

# Omnipotent Power

Heavenly Father:

In reverence of your omnipotent power and the Holy Spirit that the Risen Jesus gave to His Disciples, we praise you ceaselessly.

As we remember the cost of your love for us embodied in your Son's cross, we ask you to bless these elements upon this Table of our Lord so that we may know the fullness of The Kingdom that you have bestowed upon us.

By the Holy Spirit, may we see more clearly your grace, experience more clearly your love, and accept your counsel through prayer and supplication.

We ask this in the name of your Son, Jesus. Amen.

# Presence of the Risen Christ

Heavenly Father:

Thank you for uniting us at your Table
And granting us the presence of the Risen Christ.

Bless these elements of bread and cup
That we might have life.
In the power of your Spirit,
Let us strengthen one another to serve others.

Through these gifts of Joy and Hope
Increase our love for one another and
Let us share our faith, our hope,
And our love with our neighbors,
Our debtors and our enemies.

As we partake of these elements,
Let us hold in our hearts those in need of your care.

We pray in the name of our host, Jesus Christ. Amen.

## Voice of Your Song

Heavenly Father:

As we come to this Table of grace,
We come with grateful thanksgiving for your Son's
Merciful sacrifice and ask for your blessing upon these gifts of life.

Grant, O God, that the ears which have heard
The voice of your song will interpret the voices
Of clamor and offer peace,

That the eyes which have seen your great love
May behold your blessed hope,

That the tongues which have sung your praise
May speak your truth,

That the feet which have walked your courts
Remain to walk in the light on a foundation firm,

And the ones who will taste the life-giving elements of bread and cup,
This morning, be restored to newness of life.

We pray in the name of your Son, Jesus. Amen.[105]

# Faithful to Your Will

Eternal God, you call your people to feast at the Table of Jesus Christ.

We thank you for the presence of Christ and ask for your blessing on the gifts we are about to receive.

By the power of your Holy Spirit, keep us faithful to your will, strengthen our faith, increase our love for one another, and send us forth in courage and peace, rejoicing in the power of that same Spirit.

We ask in the name of your Son. Amen.[106]

# Rejoice in Our Salvation

Heavenly Father:

We thank you for the miracle of life, an abundant life here on earth, and an eternal life with you in Heaven.

We thank you for your Son's victory on the cross and the newness of our lives on this Easter day.

As we come to your Holy Table this morning, we come in awe of the great mercy by which you have bestowed upon us a new birth into a living hope through the resurrection of your Son from the dead.

We give thanks for these elements, symbols of the body and blood of Christ given for us and ask for your blessing on this sacred meal. As we partake of them, let us have eyes that look upon your grace and rejoice in our salvation. Let our eyes be opened afresh to the living presence of your Risen Son, Jesus, in our midst.

Lift us by your Holy Spirit to live thankfully and generously with all those whom you love. All for your glory, do we pray in Jesus' name. Amen.

# The Heavens Have Opened

Heavenly Father:

The Heavens have opened, and a star shines its light. As the Angel Gabriel rests, we can hear Heaven's angels singing. The prophets have done their work. We see that your Son has come.

In our hope-filled gaze into the manger, we are grateful witnesses to your Son's saving grace. We see the meek coming in trust. The persecuted ask for protection; the sinful, forgiveness; the lonely, companionship; the outcast, a home; and the lame, healing.

Because of your grace, we, too, have heard the Angel. We, like the wise men, have seen the light of the star over Bethlehem. We, too, have traveled to the manger to witness your newborn son, Jesus. We, too, have come knowing that by the Angel's cry and by that star overhead, You have given each one of us a great hope through your promise full of grace to save mankind.

Only You knew what it would take: the painful sacrifice of your Son on a cross. You shed your mercy upon us by sending your Son in our place for the wiping away of our sin by the sacrifice of your sinless Son. You have spared and forgiven us!

Your Son, Jesus, has set a Table before us. We ask your blessing upon these elements we are about to receive. In grateful remembrance, we, in communion with Jesus, share His broken bread and cup poured out for covenant and new life in Him. We pray in your Son's name. Amen.

# Fourth of July Weekend

Oh God,

On this Fourth of July weekend, we are thankful for a country's freedom, blessing, and justice, guaranteeing our life, liberty, and the pursuit of happiness.

We are keenly aware of the protections afforded to us by our men and women in uniform and their sacrifices to our country. We pray this day for their safety.

As we come to the Lord's Table, we ask your blessing on these elements before us. We are keenly aware of Your gift of Christ and the freedom He has set before us through His sacrificial death and resurrection. We are deeply thankful that Christ has set us free, "not from some human slavery or tyrannical authority... not for a political freedom or a freedom of the flesh but for a theological freedom."[107]. Because of the gift of your Son, our conscience is free and joyful, unafraid of the wrath to come, living as servants in your Kingdom. In this freedom, your mercy is ever before us.

"5 STAND fast therefore in the liberty wherewith Christ hath made us free, and be not entangled again with the yoke of bondage."[108]

In this time of trial, "of watching and waiting, holding tightly to You seems the best place to be as we forebear with one another. Holding tightly to each other, we raise Christ among us"[109] Knowing Your glorious Kingdom is both near and far and the heavens, themselves, tell of Your glory.

"15 For ye have not received the spirit of bondage again to fear; but ye have received the Spirit of adoption, whereby we cry, Abba, Father. 16 The Spirit itself beareth witness with our spirit, that we are the children of God:"[110]

We pray that the fears we feel today are taken away by Your grace, and we pray that our faith will be patient and grateful.

We pray in the name of your son, Jesus. Amen.

# To See You in Glory

Loving and faithful God, you have called us to feast at the Table of Christ Jesus. We give thanks for the bread and cup upon this Table and for the privilege and possibility of life itself. We give you thanks for granting us the presence of Christ.

You gave us your Son, Jesus, the Risen Christ, in order that we might see you in glory and ourselves in relationship to you. We are your children by your grace. You offer us your unconditional love from which we can never be separated through Christ Jesus, our Lord.

We ask your blessing upon these sacred gifts. We thank you for the spiritual food we are about to receive.

We sing to your relationship with us full of grace and love. Your Son opened our door to you in mercy and sacrifice so we would change our worldly ways to fellowship with you. Let justice roll on like a river, righteousness like a never-failing stream!

We are awakened to your creation in reverence and share a sense of wonder for all that is before us.

By the power of the Holy Spirit, keep us faithful to the will of Jesus. Go with us to the streets, to our homes, and to our place of labor and leisure, that whether gathered or scattered, we may be the servant church of the servant Christ.

We are blessed beyond measure for the lives you have given us in communion with others in Heaven and on Earth, through Christ for forevermore. Enable us to express our oneness with your larger family wherever life takes us.

We pray in the name of your Son, Jesus. Amen.

## Voices

Gracious God:

As the light of the world shines across this Table, may we rise toward your light like grain and be entwined like a vine in communion. You have created us in the image of your Risen Son, whom we remember as we are around this Table. With grateful hearts, we ask for your continuing blessing as you shape us more perfectly into that image.

We give thanks for this gathered family of faith, for this church home that tends, nurtures, and sends us out, and for every person who has helped to fashion us more fully into the people you desire us to be.

We thank you for receiving us in Hope and Love and for granting us the presence of Christ.

We humbly ask your blessing on these elements we are about to receive. May our lives be changed by what is manifest in broken bread and cup poured out.

As we receive these elements, so may we serve, that in our serving, we may glorify you by bringing peace, love, and justice to a thirsty world. Following Your Son's example of prayer and fasting, may we follow Him with willing hearts as new people fit for Christ's ministry to a needy world.

"Grant, Oh God, by the Holy Spirit, that our ears that have heard the voice of your song may be closed to the voice of glamour and dispute; that our eyes that have seen your great love may behold your blessed hope; that our tongues that have sung your praise may speak your truth; and that our feet that have walked your courts may walk in regions of light; and that our bodies that will taste your living bread and cup may continue to be restored to the newness of life."[111]

As Christ's ambassadors, we pray that we may bear witness to others regarding the ways of your Kingdom through the living Christ.

Glory be to you, Oh God. We ask this in Jesus' Name. Amen.

# Jesus First Loved Us

Gracious God,

We thank you for the way and truth of your Son, Jesus, in which He loves us and teaches us to love you with all our heart and our neighbor as ourselves. We pray that your truth will forever be our destination and that you have yet more light and truth to break forth from your Holy Word.

We humbly ask that you bless these elements which we are about to receive. We come before you, O God, thirsting for your word and sacrament. May our hearts burn within us that we may proclaim your mighty acts and joyfully live as your people.

Your offering of hope through Jesus allows us to have hope for our lives, each other, and the world in which we live. Your Son, Jesus, teaches us to have faith so we might have courage to live as you would have us live, serving our neighbor, the hungry, and the homeless.

We dedicate our lips to be the hopeful voice of Christ to the despairing,

Our hands to reach out in Christ's name to heal the broken,

Our feet to walk with Christ to visit those who are sick or shut-in,

And our bodies to be Christ's living sacrifice to break the power of suffering.

"We are transfigured by your mercy and radically changed by your grace. We pray that the veil of mystery shall be lifted from your face and that all shall know that you are 'God with us' at our side in Jesus Christ."[112]

Thank you for your peace that surpasses all understanding and the joy that is ours through Jesus Christ. Through Christ, receive us anew as your faithful people.

We pray all these things in the name of your Son, Jesus. Amen.

# The Gifts at the Table of the Lord

Heavenly Father,

We are forever grateful for the gift of your Son. We ask your blessing on these elements we are about to receive. In reverence, we celebrate the birth of Jesus this Christmas, and we remember the cross to which He was destined to go. We remember His last supper and celebrate the gifts at this Table of the Lord. They are His gifts given to us eternally upon your Table of Eternal Life and Redeeming Grace, your Table of Unconditional Love and Living Hope, and your Table of Everlasting Peace and Unimaginable Joy. We remember the Risen Christ, our Savior, this day, and we thank Him for these gifts of bread and cup. He gives them to us for new covenant and relationship with You, full of mercy and compassion. We are truly blessed. Amen.

# Chapter 3

# Offertory Invitations

EACH OF YOU SHOULD give what you have decided in your heart to give, not reluctantly or under compulsion, for God loves a cheerful giver. And God is able to bless you abundantly, so that in all things at all times, having all that you need, you will abound in every good work. As it is written:

> "7 Every man according as he purposeth in his heart, *so let him give;* not grudgingly, or of necessity: for God loveth a cheerful giver. 8 And God *is* able to make all grace abound toward you; that ye, always having all sufficiency in all *things*, may abound to every good work..."[113]

# Easter Sunrise, As We Stand in His Glorious Victory

This morning, by the resurrection of Jesus, evil and death have been conquered. These are the most wonderful gifts of life for us now and forever. As we stand in His glorious victory, may we come together to share gifts of our own as we are able:

Gifts that will spread good will to all within reach,
gifts that will turn fear to love,
anxiety to blessed assurance,
despair to joy, and
doubt to rock-solid faith.

Doing so, we will offer gifts of steadfast love and a firm foundation to those who are less fortunate, hungry, and homeless. Our living Risen Savior is with us as we share His love and care for all people.

## Ascribe to the Lord

From the time of the Old Testament, hear these words:

From Psalms:

"7 Give unto the LORD, O ye kindreds of the people, give unto the Lord glory and strength. 8 Give unto the LORD the glory *due unto* his name: bring an offering, and come into his courts."[114]

From 1 Chronicles:

"29 Give unto the LORD the glory *due* unto his name: bring an offering, and come before him: worship the LORD in the beauty of holiness."[115]

And from Deuteronomy:

"17 Every man *shall give* as he is able, according to the blessing of the LORD thy God which he hath given thee."[116]

From the New Testament, hear the words of the Apostle Paul from 2 Corinthians:

"7 Every man according as he purposeth in his heart, *so let him give*; not grudgingly, or of necessity: for God loveth a cheerful giver."[117]

And from the Acts, Paul reminds us to remember the words of Jesus:

"It is more blessed to give than to receive."[118]

Gracious and sacrificial giving is God's way. And He is telling us it is our way also. As he tells us, we know it to be His true word. Give your gifts today as you understand. God will bless you for it.

# Gifts That Don't Come in Boxes

After hearing Katie's sermon on the Sunday of Labor Day weekend about her special doll in a box and her weaving the story to gifts of seeing Jesus in new ways and picking up our cross and following Jesus, I realize we have some very large and wonderful gifts that just don't come in boxes.

In the book of Job, the question is asked:

"Hast thou commanded the morning since thy days; *and* caused the dayspring to know his place."[119]

This question alone reminds us of such gifts as:

> The gifts of our Heavenly Father, His Risen Son, and the Holy Spirit.

> The gifts of life and breath, of brother or sister as family and communion  with each other.

> The gifts of Heaven and Earth.

> The gifts of faith, hope, love, grace, peace, and joy.

> The good news brought by cross and empty tomb.

> The gifts of the resurrection and eternal life that tell us that there is no loss in God.

We all have received gifts in boxes for all manner of occasion. I would submit that all our gifts come from God. There is no gift given by God or given freely by us that does not come from Him.

He gives us a relationship with Him and the ability to return to him. He gives us neighbor, the charge to love him, and the wonder to nurture that relationship. Even with gifts in boxes. He has sent us out into the world to do His work. The gifts we have received along the way are for our edification and growth.

The task before us here is to give back to God. Give back. Buildup. And hold tightly His family that we have here. Give back to God. For I know the gifts we give today will multiply with His blessing, His love, and His care.

# Thanksgiving: He Gives Us Our Christian Identity

The gift of God, the Heavenly Father: the gift of His Son, Jesus, and His cross, and through baptism, the bestowing of the Holy Spirit are the gifts of life that make us who we are.

They give us our Christian identity and our relationship within the body of Christ and with others. We know that the wonderful gifts that flow from this triune God are too numerous to count, too awesome not to move us to sheer joy, and too lovely not to embrace and share with others in blessed thankfulness and prayer.

In sharing all these gifts, we bring the life of the Father and His Son to others and enliven the lives of all people one at a time and in community. It is what Jesus asks us to do.

We know His Love, His Hope, His grace, and His peace are meant to be compassionately shared, and if we do so, for us, what is reaped is true joy and a strong faith and relationship with all peoples.

As you give your gifts this morning in this spirit, know that the Lord, our God, does bless our gifts for the further expression of His Kingdom and love among people everywhere.

# The Gifts We Give to God

At retreat this past October, we as a congregation explored the gifts all around us—the gifts we give each other, the gifts we give to God, and the gifts God gives to us.

On that Saturday, during our Communion service, it was a Christian sister who reminded us that our giving is always rooted in blessed thankfulness to God—particularly for the bountiful gifts our Heavenly Father pronounced good long ago and continually bestows upon us. Gifts from God suggest the tangible and intangible nature of the miracle of our existence and daily life, all that is around us in the gifted plan of the Father, and all that is within and through us in the gifted Spirit of His Son.

Such gifts are beautiful, breathtaking, and surprising. They are too wondrous to fathom, too blessed not to soften a stony heart, and too numerous to count.

For "all things bright and beautiful" and "all things wise and wonderful,"[120] we are continually amazed and grateful this day.

Let our giving to God today be gifts given to His Son as at the manger: a giving back for all that He so lovingly has provided for us.

Most assuredly, we will be surprised by the gifts we give.

Let us be forever thankful and let us give as we are able with our hearts wide open as Jesus would have us do.

# To Be Rich Is Not How Much You Have

Listen to these words from Second Corinthians:

"9 For ye know the grace of our Lord Jesus Christ, that, though he was rich, yet for your sakes he became poor, that ye through his poverty might be rich."[121]

If we walk beside Jesus, I know we will find ourselves surrounded by such grace, for I know in faith that to be rich is not how much you have or where you are going or even who or what you are. Rich is recognizing who you have beside you.

So, as you give your gifts this morning for the furtherance of this community and the worldwide church, give as if you are the richest person on earth, knowing what Jesus, who is by your side, has done for you. And then ask the living God through His Holy Spirit to multiply the effect of your gifts on the stranger, the poor, the hungry, and the broken-hearted so they, too, may become rich in faith.

# True Bread of Life

Jesus, the Heavenly-born Son, points to the Father who welcomes you home. Jesus' way will mend you so that you will hear Him say, "Thy faith hath made thee whole."[122] Jesus knows your need for His Father's mercy. He will keep you humble; with this knowledge, you can always turn to your Father, who will keep you joyful. The Father will not forsake you, allowing you to remain steadfast. Jesus will teach you the way to go. His hold on you will be firm but gentle. Walk with Jesus, and you will find a song in your heart that you will sing in thankfulness to Him who brought you home to your Father.

In this light, as we consider the gifts that we give this morning, let us do it in the spirit of Paul's message in Romans about God's gifts to us:

"8 Or he that exhorteth, on exhortation: he that giveth, *let him do it* with simplicity; he that ruleth, with diligence; he that showeth mercy, with cheerfulness."[123]

For the sake of Jesus, let us give our gifts to our God as we are able.

## You Are No Longer Strangers

Hear Paul's words from Ephesians:

"19 Now therefore ye are no more strangers and foreigners, but fellow citizens with the saints, and of the household of God; 20 And are built upon the foundation of the apostles and prophets, Jesus Christ himself being the chief corner *stone*; 21 In whom all the building fitly framed together groweth unto a holy temple in the Lord: 22 In whom ye also are builded together for a habitation of God through the Spirit."[124]

We all have home here in a physical church building that allows us to come to Sunday service each week and set aside time to worship in the spiritual home that is in this space.

With our gifts this morning, let us take care of this physical church house so that for all who enter, we can dwell together in our spiritual home with singing and joy for the love of our Lord.

# For You Were Bought with a Price

From 1 Corinthians:

"19 What! know ye not that your body is the temple of the Holy Ghost *which is* in you, which ye have of God, and ye are not your own? 20 For ye are bought with a price: therefore glorify God in your body, and in your spirit, which are God's."[125]

This verse is telling us that we belong to God and all our gifts come from God. God is the largest influence in what we do, think, say, and pray through the living Christ. We know this to be true.

Jesus' death is the price paid through God's mercy for our freedom in our new life.

Let us give back cheerfully, knowing that this freedom given to us is precious and worth all the effort we can muster to support the living Kingdom of God through Christ's church with our gifts. Give as you are able.

# Gifts of a Savior

We have come from the Table of the Lord as free agents of Christ's reconciling love. Our hearts have been refreshed by the gifts of a Savior. May what we bring as an offering this morning enrich those in need.[126]

Let us remember the words of Christ Jesus:

"It is more blessed to give than to receive."[127]

Give as you are able.

# If You Fear Change

The other day, Mary and I were in a local restaurant, and after we bought our meals at the counter, we put our tip in the tip jar before we sat down.

There was a message on the jar that read: "If you fear change, leave it here."

As far as pocket change for the one in need, I sometimes fear not giving enough. Worldly change, on the other hand, is plentiful.

In this world, we will always be faced with change. Our reaction to it is most important.

Our Lord tells us:

"25 Therefore I say to you, Take no thought for your life, what ye shall eat, or what ye shall drink; nor yet for your body, what ye shall put on. Is not the life more than meat, and the body than raiment?"[128]

Further in Matthew's Gospel, He teaches:

"34 Take therefore no thought for the morrow: for the morrow shall take thought for the things of itself. Sufficient unto the day *is* the evil thereof."[129]

As far as tomorrow is concerned, I know that God is already there.

The world's change involves a certain amount of trouble. Jesus, in Matthew's Gospel, is telling us that.

Yet, in the present day, I'm sure we can do something about it. That's where our resources come in. And while we are at it, let's anticipate the Lord's transformational change that we can offer.

We know that at this Table, Jesus offers us covenant, forgiveness, healing, and new life in our living before God. Let's offer it to others. Let's put ourselves and the change we offer in God's hands.

As God transforms us, we will be able to offer God's hope to those who fear the change they see in the world, and we will transform their lives as well. Give as you are able.

# Self-Offering of Jesus Christ

God presents us with the costly self-offering of Jesus Christ, who has claimed us and set us free. Our Savior is a Holy gift of God from God.

The Christian life is marked by the offering of oneself to God through Jesus. We are led to respond by offering to God our lives, our spiritual gifts, and our abilities to share in God's glory in Christ.

The offering of our tithes, time, and talent in worship is an act of self-dedication, and it expresses our thanksgiving to God, the giver of life.

This is our affirmation as Christ's disciples of our commitment to be stewards of all creation: to share the Word and to care for all people, to share God's gifts with those in need, and to share our common bond in the body of Christ.

Let us bring our gifts so that the ministry of this church will be a growing, vibrant witness to God's love. Gather our gifts together and offer them to God in gratitude and praise. Give as you are able.

# The Form of Two Coins

Several years ago, I was contemplating what life should look like "when Jesus is in the room." I know this is God's house, where we come to worship Him, and the Spirit of Jesus lives in all of us. And further, Jesus has assured us:

"20 For where two or three are gathered together in my name, there am I in the midst of them."[130]

If Jesus is in this room, the warmth can be felt. Hope can blossom. Love will surround. Good will spread. Freedom is shared. Peace is here. Faith is sustained. Grace will abound. Thankfulness will multiply. Understanding will heal. Prayers are central to our experience. The sick will be made well. Compassion will engage. The children will be made whole. Hands will hold. And loving hearts will rest.

Kind eyes, compassionate ears, loving hearts, and strong arms will accomplish His will. We know that Jesus has taught us that it is our response to need that is important to us as His followers. In this regard, this morning, it's what we put in the offering that remains important. Need is there. It's etched in the center of the plate.

So, Jesus encourages us to put Hope, Promise, Prayers, Compassion, Bread, Understanding, Goodwill, and Blessing in the offering.

For each of us, the gift may only be in the form of two small coins with a prayer, yet the gift is God's love for our neighbor and stranger who need our care. Give as you are able.

# The Joyful Effect of Gift-Giving

This Christmas, we all know that the joyful effect of gift-giving cannot be calculated for the giver or the receiver. Freely given gifts can be surprising to both, especially when you know Santa is coming to town. One Christmas, many years ago, my mother shared with me a very simple but meaningful statement about Santa Claus:

"To believe in making wishes
and have faith they can come true,
To believe that you can find some joy
in everything you do,
To believe in giving gladly
for no reason, just because,
To believe in love...that's what it means
to believe in Santa Claus."

The night before last, I am sure Santa's elves were busying themselves to make glad the heart of children all over the world. That's how Santa does it. Well, Jesus has all of us—our hearts and minds and our belief in giving gladly.

Once again, kind eyes, compassionate ears, loving hearts, and strong arms will accomplish God's will this Christmas season in all manner of giving. Whether it be your tithes or talent, your kindness in your actions or speaking, your goodwill, or a prayer behind the gift, it is your sharing with others that counts. Your manner of giving may be worth more than the gift.

Spontaneous, heart-felt, and freely given gifts. If we think about it, that is what Jesus has given us our life long. This Christmas season, let us turn ourselves toward the hungry, the thirsty, the stranger, the naked, the sick. This morning, let us give with our hearts wide open, as Jesus would have us do for the furtherance of His Kingdom here on earth. Surely, we will be surprised by the result for ourselves and those we serve. Give as you are able.

# Strangers Becoming Neighbors

When I first came to Church as an adult over thirty years ago, I had a lot of questions, and I was suffering. You might say I was the stranger entering the House of worship; the congregation, upon first encounter, were strangers to me. But warmth is what I found. Over the years in the church, I have learned of the beauty of Jesus' birth, His teachings, the meaning of the Lord's Table, His cruci-fixion, and His resurrection and ascension. I learned that I could have an authentic relationship with our living God and that I could not be separated from His love in Christ Jesus. Jesus taught me of the greatest commandment, which is:

"27 Thou shalt love the Lord thy God with all thy heart, and with all thy soul, and with all thy strength, and with all thy mind; and thy neighbor as thyself."[131]

When I give at the time the offering is passed, I think of the love I have for the stranger who might, in fact, become my neighbor and is in need. Our love for all of them is reflected in the offering. These strangers, whether poor, disenfranchised, homeless, or hungry, have a lot of questions and are suffering. Jesus teaches:

"42 Give to him that asketh thee, and from him that would borrow of thee turn not thou away."[132]

The gift in the offering this morning may be for strangers. Yet, I suggest it's not. Our supporting the Safe Haven Ministry is a good example of strangers becoming neighbors through our ministry of love, care, and much needed food. These strangers have become neighbors. Strangers will become neighbors through the transformative action of giving to the offering. Our gifts may open church doors to those who question and to those who suffer. And neighbors will be found for us to love as ourselves, and warmth will be found. Give as you are able.

## Let Jesus Influence you

Jesus gave Himself on a cross for our sake, and when resurrected, He gave us the Holy Spirit and our ability to recognize our Heavenly Father and live with him through that Spirit. As we pray the prayer he taught us, we pray for God's will to be done, not ours. He tells us to love God with all our heart and love one another and our neighbor as ourselves. When we act in this way, we are helping God's children. And further, He asks us to help the least of these. Remember, the Lord is the largest influence in our lives. Let Him influence you. He is asking us to respond with love to the needs of all His children. Give as you are able.

# Give With Kindness

"2 Be not forgetful to entertain strangers: for thereby some have entertained angels unawares."[133]

As you give your gifts this morning, give with kindness. Give with a smile. Say a prayer for all those whom these gifts will support. Your prayers will be behind the gifts. Good will, good intention, and love will be behind the gifts. Behind these tangible gifts are the dreams of the intangible. These tangible gifts will support the intangible ones among all those we call brothers and sisters, though they are strangers. Let us remember the familiar biblical passage in Matthew:

"35 For I was ahungered, and ye gave me meat: I was thirsty, and ye gave me drink: I was a stranger, and ye took me in:"[134]

"7 Wherefore receive ye one another, as Christ also received us, to the glory of God."[135]

Give as you are able.

# Wealth

"We live in God's grace. Christ is God's grace, mercy, righteousness, truth, wisdom, power, comfort, and salvation given to us by God without any merit on our part."[136] Thus, as Christians, we are blessed as wealthy beyond measure.

Whether it be your tithes or talent, your kindness in your actions or speaking your goodwill, or a prayer behind the gift, it is your wealth you share with others. It may be your manner of giving that is the gift.

Christ loves a cheerful giver, so give whatever that may be. Give to the hungry and needy. Let your own love for Christ stir you to give generously. Your tangible gifts will support the intangible ones for stranger, neighbor, brother, and sister alike.

Bring your offering in response to God's grace. Christ calls us to give our commitment. With our voices, we will sing His praises. With our hands, we will care for the suffering. All we have, we return to the Lord, for He endows us with bountiful and beautiful gifts of wealth for us to share.

# Chapter 4

# Offertory Prayers

## Spiritual gift

Heavenly Father:

Thanks be to you for your spiritual gift and grace of your Son, Jesus. As we, like the wise men, present these gifts, we sincerely pray that, whether our gifts come from abundance or portion, they are given as an outpouring from our hearts in your service as we recognize the true need of others.

Just as we have been blessed by Holy gifts of communion, Lord, we ask that you bless these gifts we offer in the forbearance of your Kingdom here on earth.

In our hope-filled gaze into the manger, we, too, witness your promise fulfilled. We see the meek coming in trust. The persecuted ask for protection; the sinful, forgiveness; the lonely, companionship; the outcast, a home; and the lame, healing.

Our gifts are given for those in need. As we have been given many gifts in one Spirit, we pray that we all give as we are able. In Jesus' name, we ask. Amen.

# Let Our Faith be Shared

Heavenly Father:

Bless these gifts we give this morning so that in our prayer for community here and beyond our doors, these gifts will bring needful things to the needy, food to the hungry, and clothing to the poor.

In the words of a hymn, we have sung:

These gifts of currency be love and kindness our law.

"Community of Christ through whom the word must sound—cry out for justice and for peace the whole world round: disarm the powers that war and all that can destroy turn bombs to bread, and tears of anguish into joy."[137]

May these gifts remind us of the song in our hearts as we share our song with those unfamiliar or foreign, those sick or aching, and those less fortunate or different from ourselves.

"...our currency be love and kindliness our law, our food and faith be shared as one forevermore."[138]

In the name of Jesus, we ask. Amen.

# From Your Bounty

Heavenly Father:

Just as we have been blessed by Holy gifts of Communion this morning, we ask that you bless these gifts we offer for the furtherance of your Kingdom here on earth.

These gifts are given sincerely from the bounty you have set before us. We pray ceaselessly that our gifts to you will spread blessings of love and care to all your children in need.

We pray this in the name of your Son, Jesus. Amen.

# Giving Can Reach the Ends of the Earth

Heavenly Father:

We offer these gifts in reverence and in joy
for the furtherance of this and your wider church.

We know your voice can add majesty to our singing.
You bless us beyond measure.
Your hand holds us in compassionate grace.

As we walk humbly with you
and love you with our whole heart, soul, and mind,
We know that in our giving,
the love with which you love us
can reach the ends of the earth.

As we offer these gifts back to you this morning,
we ask that you multiply them
as your Son multiplied loaves and fishes in love
on a mountainside for so many
long ago.

In this way, we pray that you will help us always
to give abundantly to those in need.

We ask this in the name of your Son, Jesus. Amen.

# Grace-filled Care of Others

Heavenly Father:

Just as we have been blessed by these gifts of Communion this morning, we ask that you bless these gifts we offer for the furtherance of your Kingdom on earth.

We pray that, by our hands in yours, these gifts, through this church, will reach and strengthen those most in need—the homeless, the hungry, and the poor among us.

Let us share these gifts in the care of others as Jesus would have us do.

We ask this in the name of your Son. Amen.

# Holy Gifts of Life

Heavenly Father:

We have received holy gifts of life and breath from you our whole life long. We have been surrounded by your gifts that surprise, heal, and sustain us. Some have been given to us in necessity for our growth. We have been blessed beyond measure.

Through the cross of your Son, you have given us the grace to see that our lives are holy in your sight, hearts that turn toward need in this world, and hands to respond to it. You have opened our eyes to recognize your love in the middle of our response.

As each of our gifts is given this morning, we pray that they are raised by your blessing for the furtherance of your Kingdom here on earth.

We pray in the name of your Son, Jesus. Amen.

# Life is a Sacred Gift

Heavenly Father:

In your hands, you have revealed to us that life is a sacred gift. We know that all the wonderful gifts that flow from you are too numerous to count, too awesome not to move us to sheer joy, and too lovely not to embrace and share with others in blessed thankfulness and prayer.

In sharing all your gifts, we pray that we may bring your majesty and the life of your Son to others and enliven the lives of all peoples one at a time and in community.

This is what your Son, Jesus, asks us to do. We know your Love, your Hope, your Grace, and your Peace are meant to be compassionately shared, and if we do so, for us, what is reaped is true joy and a strong faith in relationship with all people.

As we give our gifts this morning, in this spirit, we pray that you will bless our gifts for the further expression of your Kingdom and your love among people everywhere. We ask this in the name of your Son, Jesus. Amen.

# Tangible and Intangible

Heavenly Father,

We offer these gifts to you this morning, remembering that in this place, our gifts support the tangible and the intangible for our lives together, for the stranger, for the less fortunate, the homeless, and the hungry.

And as each gift is given, we know there is blessing. For we know, behind each gift is love. Behind each gift is good will. And behind each gift are the dreams of this church shared with welcomed strangers thereby entertaining angels unaware. We welcome one another as Christ welcomed us home by calling us brothers and sisters.

We pray in the Name of your Son, Jesus. Amen.

## To Serve Your Kingdom

Heavenly Father:

We bring these, our gifts, before you
and ask your blessing upon us
as we strive to serve your Kingdom
with our time, our talent, and our tithe.

With gratitude for your Son's teaching,
we dedicate our lips to be the hopeful voice to the despairing,
our hands to reach out in Christ's name to heal the broken,
our feet to walk with Christ to visit those who are sick and shunned,
and our bodies to be the living witness to Christ's sacrifice saving
people worldwide, one person at a time.

We ask this in the name of your Son, Jesus. Amen.[139]

# Signs of Our Labor

Heavenly Father:

We offer these gifts in reverence and in joy for the furtherance of this church and your wider kingdom .

We offer these signs of our labor for sustenance and healing for those within the fold of this church and the community beyond our doors.

We humbly pray in the name of your Son, Jesus. Amen.

# Life and Breath

Creator God:

You have given us the holy gifts of life and breath. We have been surrounded by your gifts of earth and sky each night and every day.

Your gifts of love and grace have nourished in us heavenly peace. Your gifts have surprised us, healed us, and sustained us. Some have been offered to us as necessity for the joyful growth of our spiritual faith.

Through the cross of your Son, you have given us the grace to see that our lives are Holy in your sight. We have been blessed beyond measure.

We now have hearts that have turned toward your Kingdom in service to the less fortunate, the homeless, and the hungry. We have seen the wideness of your mercy and the fullness of your love.

We ask for your blessing upon these gifts this morning, and we pray that by your blessing, these gifts will multiply to abundance for those in need. We ask this in the name of your Son, Jesus. Amen.

## Easter: We Have Seen the Lord

Heavenly Father:

We rejoice this morning that we, like Mary Magdalene, have experienced the resurrected Lord. We give thanks to you for this most beautiful of gifts, assuring us of life everlasting.

As we stand firm in the resurrection light this morning, we offer our gifts back to you in joyful gratitude in service to your kingdom. We ask that you richly bless these gifts, that their effect might be multiplied among those in need.

May we continue to discover anew our role in reaching out to those who are brokenhearted, to those who are hungry and homeless, and to those who are crushed in spirit until that time when the daybreak of Christ's love envelops and sustains all people on the earth.

Jesus, the Christ, is risen for all! Let us be glad in this good news! We ask this in the name of your Son. Amen.

# We, Like the Wise Men

Creator God:

Thanks be to you for your spiritual gift and for the grace of your Son, Jesus. As we, like the wise men, present these gifts this morning, we sincerely pray that they are given as an outpouring from our hearts in your service as we recognize the true need of others.

Our gifts are given for those in need. As we have been given many gifts in one Spirit, we give as we are able. We ask that you richly bless these gifts for the glory of your Kingdom so they might be multiplied among those in need.

We continually offer praise to you, and for ourselves to be mindful not to neglect to do good and share what we have with the less fortunate, hungry, and homeless. We pray this in your Son's name. Amen.

# Indescribable Gifts

Merciful God:

Thanks be to you for your indescribable gifts. We sincerely pray that our gifts are given as an outpouring from our hearts as we recognize the true need of others. We pray that we have all given as we are able. We ask for your blessing on these gifts to the glory of your Kingdom. We continually offer a sacrifice of praise to you. We strive to do good and to share what we have in ministry with the less fortunate, hungry, and homeless. Amen.

# Acknowledgments

REVEREND CHARLES WILDMAN AND Reverend Phil White from Rock Spring Congregational United Church of Christ and Reverend Jack Austin, Reverend Kathleen Kline Moore, and Reverend Steven Moore from First Christian Church of Falls Church, Christian Church (Disciples of Christ), have been true gifts to me. I have journaled for over 40 years. Early in that experience, Reverend Wildman and Reverend White both encouraged me. Reverend White encouraged me to find out what was in my own mind and heart concerning Jesus. Reverend Wildman told me, "In our deepest despair lies the seed of our strongest faith."

Reverend Jack Austin told me that when Jesus said, "It is finished," from the cross, He was telling us that we are saved by His cross, and through Him, nothing can separate us from the love of God. Reverend Kathleen Kline Moore invited me to be an elder ten years ago, which has been a true honor. She told the congregation, "Repentance and forgiveness of sin is the mark of a resurrection faith." Regarding my illness, Reverend Steven Moore gave me hope, saying: "We can be healed without a cure because Jesus heals, and He is eternal."

Their guidance, care, and compassion have allowed me to grow as a Christian in the fellowship of the church. All of them have helped me to listen to and accept the voice of God and to seek guidance through the process of prayer for what He wants me to be and to do. They have taught me to see all that God does with me and through me in the world with excitement. They have helped me realize the mystery of God and His profound gift of forgiving love. They have taught me that faith is lived with patience and gratitude. All these ministers have been a blessing to me.

Jesus forgives me from His cross, wipes my slate clean, and redeems me. The Father God created me. His Son, Jesus, redeems me, and I am thankful. I am to love God and to love others as they are.

# Bibliography

First Christian Church of Falls Church, Falls Church, Virginia.

Chambers, Oswald. The Complete Works of Oswald Chambers c. 2000 by Oswald Chambers Publications Association Limited, Discovery House Publishers, Box 3566, Grand Rapids MI 49501. pp. 343, 507, 510, 560, 748, 1228.

James Reimann Ed. My Utmost for His Highest. October 28. Discovery House Publishers, Grand Rapids, Michigan. 1992.

Merton, Thomas. New Seeds of Contemplation. Abbey of Gethsemane, New Directions Publishing Corp. New York, New York. 1961 p. 75.

Saint Francis of Assisi (Public Domain).

Bach, Johann Sebastian. "Christmas Oratorio" BWV 248 1734 (Public Domain).

Chalice Hymnal. Chalice Press, Saint Louis, Missouri 1995.

Sheen, Fulton J. Life of Christ. Doubleday. New York, New York 1990 p. 26.

De Caussade, Jean-Pierre. The Joy of Full Surrender. Paraclete Press, Brewster, Massachusetts. 2008 pp. 13 & 17.

Wildman, Reverend Charles. Sermon, Rock Spring Congregational, UCC. Arlington, Virginia.

Small, Thomas. Personal Communication

Unknown speaker at McLean Presbyterian Church, McLean, Virginia circa 2001.

Haynes, Lashaun. Personal Communication.

Entry in the 1943 journal of Mrs. Josephine Lehmann Miser.

Saint Simeon. Public Domain.

Wildman, Reverend Charles. Communion. Rock Spring Congregational UCC. Arlington, Virginia.

Luther, Martin. Public Domain.

Kirk, James G. When We Gather. Geneva Press, Louisville, Kentucky. 2001 pp. 280 & 340.

Alexander, Cecil Francis. Public Domain 1948.

All Biblical References are set forth in the 1611 King James Version, American Bible Society and the Bible is in the Public Domain.

# Author Bio

## Wendel L. Miser

I grew up in the same home in New England with my brother Jim. I was, however, preoccupied with my twin brother, Andy, in our formative years and through high school. It was in high school that I met my wife, Mary, marrying her in September 1972, after finishing at Cornell

College in Mt. Vernon, Iowa in June of 1972.

I received a Master of Science degree from the University of Illinois in 1975, after studying Zoology and Limnology. After graduate school, I worked with Mary's father in his painting business before accepting a position in the Office of Solid Waste at the United States Environmental Protection Agency in Washington, D.C. in 1977.

I began with their program of pesticide disposal for a short time and then became a project officer, managing the program side for the Agency's contract office. Working with the contract officer, I helped the staff with contract pre-award and post-award requirements for their work. In that capacity, I was involved for 23 years in the development of a nationwide hazardous waste management program. Subsequently, I moved to the Office's municipal waste program that was promoting recycling and sustainability programs at the time.

While not at work during the latter half of my career, I became interested in singing. For the better part of 20 years, I was involved with the New Dominion Chorale and the National Men's Chorus in the Washington, D.C. area. The New Dominion Chorale featured works by the Great Masters, while the National Men's Chorus showcased works specially arranged by the music director for the Chorus. Memorable concerts were given at the National Cathedral and the Kennedy Center as well as the National Gallery of Art, Washington, D.C. For six years, I served on the Board of Directors of the National Men's Chorus, assisting with grant activities.

I live with my wife in Arlington, Virginia and our two cats, Linus and Madeleine. We attend church regularly in Falls Church, Virginia. I have kept a faith-based journal for 40 years. In overcoming schizophrenia and finding joy, I have entered full participation in life.

# Author Bio

## James S. Miser, MD

I grew up on the East Coast of the United States with my father, mother, two younger twin brothers, and a younger sister, spending the majority of time in New England. My father was a mathematician with a PhD in this field, and he was an operations research and systems analysis professional.

My mother had a Master of Science degree in Child Development; she spent most of our formative years caring for us as we grew and developed. We were a normal family and could not know what was to befall Wendel at age 28.

I am a Pediatric Hematologist and Oncologist and have taken care of children with cancer and blood diseases for almost 50 years. I received a Bachelor of Arts degree from Dartmouth College in Hanover, New Hampshire, in 1969, majoring in Religion. While there, I also was the director of the college's acapella singing group. In the summers during high school and college, I taught tennis to children. Although I intended to be a mathematician, I decided to spend my life working with children and entered Dartmouth Medical School with the intention to be a pediatrician. I subsequently transferred to the University of Washington in Seattle, Washington, where I received a Doctor of Medicine in 1973 and trained in Pediatrics and Pediatric Hematology and Oncology.

At the beginning of my experience of caring for children with cancer, I accepted the Lord Jesus Christ as Lord and Savior of my life. This has been an important relationship for me since that time. I have worked as a Pediatric Hematologist/Oncologist at: Ohio State University; the National Institutes of Health; Mayo Clinic; the University of Washington, where I was granted the position of Professor of Pediatrics; and City of Hope National Medical Center, where I was Chairman of Pediatrics.

I also served as President and Chief Medical Officer at City of Hope National Medical Center as it developed a comprehensive cancer center.

I have authored more than 100 manuscripts and book chapters. I worked as medical director and served as Chairman of the American Board of Directors of a child rescue organization— Christian Salvation Service, in Taipei, Taiwan, serving children and women. During this time, I was also Chair Professor of Pediatrics at Taipei Medical University, where I was challenged to develop a Pediatric Hematology/Oncology program for the University.

I also served as Chairman of the Board of Directors of a Christian High School in southern California and currently serve as Chairman of the Board of Directors of a nonprofit organization supporting children with cancer and their families.

My wife Angela and I have adopted 10 children, many with significant challenges. I live in Wales with my wife and five of the children. I enjoy walking, reading, playing tennis, and singing. I attend church with my wife in the Church of Wales. The mission of my life has been to serve children, both personally and professionally, especially those with significant challenges in their lives.

I have been close to my brother, Wendel, in his journey with schizophrenia and shared the initial horror, the subsequent anxiety of the ups and downs of his experience, and now the joy of his overcoming.

It has been a privilege to travel his journey and to write this book with him.

# Endnotes

1    First Christian Church of Falls Church, Falls Church, Virginia

2    St. Matthew 26:26-28 KJV Public Domain

3    St. John 14:6 KJV Public Domain

4    Taken from The Complete Works of Oswald Chambers ® 2000 by Oswald Chambers Publications Association Limited. Used by permission of Discovery House Publishers, Box 3566, Grand Rapids MI 49501. All rights reserved. Oswald Chambers, p. 510

5    Paraphrased from the October 28th daily devotion from My Utmost For His Highest. 1992 Used by permission of Our Daily Bread Publishing.

6    St. John 6:35 KJV Public Domain

7    1 Peter 5:10 KJV Public Domain

8    St. Luke 12:7 KJV Public Domain

9    Psalm 139:16 KJV Public Domain

10   Psalm 100:3 KJV Public Domain

11   Isaiah 49:16 KJV Public Domain

12   St. Matthew 6:25 KJV Public Domain

13   Isaiah 41:10 KJV Public Domain

14   1 Peter 5:10 KJV Public Domain

15   Isaiah 44:22 KJV Public Domain

16   Ezekiel 36:26 KJV Public Domain

17   St. John 10:10 KJV Public Domain

18   St. John 14:20-24 KJV Public Domain

| | |
|---|---|
| 19 | Excerpt from New Seeds of Contemplation by Thomas Merton, copyright 1961 by The Abbey of Gethsemani, Inc. Reprinted by permission of New Directions Publishing Corp. |
| 20 | St. Mark 11:17 KJV Public Domain |
| 21 | Jeremiah 29:12 KJV Public Domain |
| 22 | Taken from The Complete Works of Oswald Chambers ® 2000 by Oswald Chambers Publications Association Limited. Used by permission of Discovery House Publishers, Box 3566, Grand Rapids MI 49501. All rights reserved. |
| 23 | Ephesians 1:13-14 KJV Public Domain |
| 24 | Attributed to St. Francis of Assisi (Public Domain) |
| 25 | St. Luke 24:32 KJV Public Domain |
| 26 | Romans 6:3-4 KJV Public Domain |
| 27 | Bach, Johann Sebastian "Christmas Oratorio" BWV 248 1734 (Public Domain) |
| 28 | St. Luke 2:10 KJV Public Domain |
| 29 | St. Luke 2:11-14 KJV Public Domain |
| 30 | St. John 3:16-17 KJV Public Domain |
| 31 | St. Luke 2:14 KJV Public Domain |
| 32 | St. Matthew 6:9 KJV Public Domain |
| 33 | St. John 19:30 KJV Public Domain |
| 34 | Chalice Hymnal Public Domain |
| 35 | St. John 20:19-22 KJV Public Domain |
| 36 | FCCFC. Season of Pentecost. Father's Day. June 21, 2015. |
| 37 | Romans 8:11 KJV Public Domain |
| 38 | St. John 1:1-5,14 KJV Public Domain |
| 39 | 1 Peter 1:3-5 KJV Public Domain |
| 40 | Romans 8:37-39 KJV Public Domain |
| 41 | Romans 12:1 KJV Public Domain |
| 42 | Ephesians 2:19-22 KJV Public Domain |
| 43 | Hebrews 13:2 KJV Public Domain |

44   St. Luke 24: 32 KJV Public Domain

45   St. John 13:35 KJV Public Domain

46   Romans 12:1 KJV Public Domain

47   Isaiah 44:22 KJV Public Domain

48   Taken from The Complete Works of Oswald Chambers ® 2000 by Oswald Chambers Publications Association Limited. Used by permission of Discovery House Publishers, Box 3566, Grand Rapids MI 49501. All rights reserved.

49   St. John 3:16-17 KJV Public Domain

50   1 Peter 1:3-5 KJV Public Domain

51   1 Peter 5:10 KJV Public Domain

52   Taken from The Complete Works of Oswald Chambers ® 2000 by Oswald Chambers Publications Association Limited. Used by permission of Discovery House Publishers, Box 3566, Grand Rapids MI 49501. All rights reserved.

53   1 Thessalonians 5:23-24 KJV Public Domain

54   1 Corinthians 6:20 KJV Public Domain

55   1 Peter 1:18-19 KJV Public Domain

56   St. Matthew 22:37-40 KJV Public Domain

57   St. Matthew 6:21 KJV Public Domain

58   Romans 5:1-5 KJV Public Domain

59   Ephesians 1:7 Public Domain

60   St. Luke 14:27 KJV Public Domain

61   St. Matthew 25:40 KJV Public Domain

62   St. Luke 17:19 KJV Public Domain

63   Sheen, Fulton J.  Life of Christ.  Doubleday, 1990, p. 26.

64   Galatians 2:20 KJV Public Domain

65   1 Corinthians 15:3-4; 21-22 KJV Public Domain

66   Micah 6:8 KJV Public Domain

67   Romans 8:1-2 KJV Public Domain

68   Taken from The Complete Works of Oswald Chambers ® 2000

by Oswald Chambers Publications Association Limited. Used by permission of Discovery House Publishers, Box 3566, Grand Rapids MI 49501. All rights reserved. p. 560.

69 St. Matthew 6:28-34 KJV Public Domain

70 The Joy of Full Surrender by Jean-Pierre De Caussade, Copyright 2008 by Paraclete Press. Used by permission of Paraclete Press. P. 13.

71 Jean-Pierre De Caussade The Joy of Full Surrender p.17

72 Wildman, Reverend Charles, Communion, Rock Spring Congregational, UCC

73 St. John 1:1, 14 KJV Public Domain

74 1 Peter 1:3 KJV Public Domain

75 Romans 8:28-33 KJV Public Domain

76 Romans 12:1-2 KJV Public Domain

77 Rev. Thomas Small, September 2003

78 Rev. Thomas Small, April 2001

79 Taken from The Complete Works of Oswald Chambers ® 2000 by Oswald Chambers Publications Association Limited. Used by permission of Discovery House Publishers, Box 3566, Grand Rapids MI 49501. All rights reserved. p.748.

80 St. Matthew 14:25-31 KJV Public Domain

81 St. Luke 12:32 KJV Public Domain

82 Psalm 23:4 KJV Public Domain

83 St. John 14:27 KJV Public Domain

84 1 John 4:18 KJV Public Domain

85 Rev. Thomas Small.

86 Unknown speaker, McLean Presbyterian Church, McLean, Virginia circa 2001

87 Lashaun Haynes personal communication.

88 Entry in the 1943 journal of Mrs. Josephine Lehmann Miser

89 Entry in the 1943 journal of Mrs. Josephine Lehmann Miser

90 2 Thessalonians 1:11-12 KJV Public Domain

91    Galatians 2:20 KJV Public Domain

92    Entry in the 1943 journal of Mrs. Josephine Lehmann Miser

93    Ephesians 2:4-6 KJV Public Domain

94    Ephesians 1:13-14 KJV Public Domain

95    St.Matthew 18:20 KJV Public Domain

96    Saint Simeon. Public Domain

97    Small, Thomas.

98    Ephesians 1:13-14 KJV Public Domain

99    Psalm 100 KJV Public Domain

100   Acts 1:8 KJV Public Domain

101   John 10:30 Public Domain

102   John 19:30 Public Domain

103   St. Matthew 22:37 and 39 KJV Public Domain

104   Used by permission from Charles Wildman.

105   Used by permission from Charles Wildman.

106   Used by permission from Charles Wildman.

107   Martin Luther, Public Domain

108   Galatians 5:1 KJV Public Domain

109   Wildman, Rev Charles.  Communion. Rock Spring Congrega-
      tional UCC, Arlington, Virginia.

110   Romans 8:15-16 KJV Public Domain

111   Used by permission from Charles Wildman.

112   When We Gather by James G. Kirk. 2001, Used by permission of
      Westminster John Knox Press, p.280.

113   2 Corinthians 9:7-8 KJV Public Domain

114   Psalm 96:7-8 KJV Public Domain

115   1 Chronicles 16:29 KJV Public Domain

116   Deuteronomy 16:17 KJV Public Domain

117   2 Corinthians 9:7 KJV Public Domain

118   The Acts 20:35 KJV Public Domain

119   Job 38:12 KJV Public Domain

120   Hymn by Cecil Francis Alexander 1948 Public Domain

121   2 Corinthians 8:9 KJV Public Domain

122   St. Luke 17:19 KJV Public Domain

123   Romans. 12:8 KJV Public Domain

124   Ephesians 2:19-22 KJV Public Domain

125   1 Corinthians 6:19-20 KJV Public Domain

126   Paraphrased from When We Gather by James G. Kirk, p. 340, 2001, Used by permission of Westminster John Knox Press.

127   The Acts 20:35 KJV Public Domain

128   St. Matthew 6:25 KJV Public Domain

129   St. Matthew 6:34 KJV Public Domain

130   St. Matthew18:20 KJV Public Domain

131   St. Luke 10:27 KJV Public Domain

132   St. Matthew 5:42 KJV Public Domain

133   Hebrews 13:2 KJV Public Domain

134   St. Matthew 25:35 KJV Public Domain

135   Romans 15:7 KJV Public Domain

136   Martin Luther, Public Domain

137   Hymn 655, verse 3 Chalice Hymnal, Chalice Press, 1995. Used by permission from Chalice Press, P.O. Box 179, St. Louis, MO 63166-0179

138   Hymn 655, verse 4 Chalice Hymnal, Chalice Press, 1995. Used by permission from Chalice Press, P.O. Box 179, St. Louis, MO 63166-0179

139   Used by permission from Reverend Charles Wildman.